The Shadow of His Hand

The Shadow of His Hand

The Dramatic Account of One Man's Quest for Fulness of Life in the Spirit

Norris L. Wogen

Bethany Fellowship, Inc.
Minneapolis, Minnesota 55438

Library of Congress Catalog Card Number 74-21059

ISBN 0-87123-533-1

The Shadow of His Hand
Norris L. Wogen

Copyright © 1974
Bethany Fellowship, Inc.
All Rights Reserved

Published by Bethany Fellowship, Inc.
6820 Auto Club Road, Minneapolis, Minnesota 55438

Printed in the United States of America

FOREWORD

There are very few men among my friends who have gained such a wide experience in so short a time in the present-day charismatic renewal of the churches as the writer of this book. In a few years I have learned to know him and trust him as a man with balanced judgment of personal, social and ecclesiastical affairs. His deep sincerity and enthusiasm in Christian life has intrigued me.

I am glad that he took the time and made the effort to write this book. He has answered wisely many of the questions that are raised by the clergy in the historic churches regarding this phenomenon of the Holy Spirit in the life of Christian communities and churches.

It has been my privilege to have him as a companion in institutional meetings and spiritual conferences in different states and in Europe. Always his personal appearance and public ministry has adorned the gospel of Jesus Christ.

Someday, multitudes will flock to the judgment seat of Christ to bear testimony to the blessings that they have received under the ministry of this faithful pastor and teacher. I firmly believe that he is one of the men in the Lutheran church whom God has called for a special ministry at such a time as this.

I trust his writings will appeal to many readers who honestly seek to know "the way, the truth, and the life" as it can be found only in the Lord Jesus Christ, Savior, Healer, Baptizer in the Holy Spirit and soon-coming Lord of lords and King of kings.

David J. du Plessis

Oakland, CA
August, 1974

PREFACE

The American Lutheran Church is made up
of 2,492,355 baptized members and has enjoyed
periods of rather striking growth. Not too many
years ago a new congregation was being added
to the denomination every eighteen days. The
home mission venture was regarded almost as
big business because it took a lot of capital to
finance the program of expansion. Trained men
were coming out of our seminaries in sufficient
numbers to provide pastors for the new congregations being established as well as to shepherd
the congregations who were mothering and fa-
thering the new ones. We could perhaps call
it a golden age in the Lutheran church. The
common characteristic that marked the clergy
was that of enthusiasm. The lay people, happy
with their leadership, supported the programs
of the Lutheran church in an exemplary manner.

Many of us were living during those days,
and we look back with longing at "the good old
days." But there came a change in the condition

of the church. The phenomenal growth was no longer the norm. Mergers, we assume, had something to do with a decline of interest and enthusiasm, but there was something more needed to explain the change. And no one, apparently, was qualified or gifted enough to explain what had taken place. Boredom and apathy were to be found, and a critical attitude developed, which served to diminish rather than increase the strength of the church. In many instances the emphasis was on the number of souls in a congregation and the number of dollars returned on the investments that could be utilized to establish yet more congregations.

To witness and be a part of a drowsy spiritual giant is not the most exciting experience a person may have. We did not want for the number of diagnosis being offered. We went the route of structural organization, new programs, new educational material, changes in liturgical forms, new hymns and hymn books, but no lever was found that could bring the Lutheran church again into high gear. One rather frightening theory appeared on the horizon that suggested that "maybe God is dead." Few believed it, if any, but we mention it here just to indicate and emphasize the seriousness of our situation.

No one was more conscious of the state of the church than the Lord of the church, and no one was more determined to make it gloriously alive! The question the Lord of the church asked the prophet Ezekiel as He placed him in the valley of dry bones was echoing again in the minds of many a man of God, "Son of man, can these bones live?" (Ezek. 37:1-3). And the response of the men who were called to lead the church was quite general, "Thou knowest, O Lord!" We had come close to exhausting the remedies that might be used to bring His church again into full bloom.

The experiences of the Lutheran church was more or less true of the rest of the bodies of Christendom with few exceptions. And the experience that was to bring renewed zeal and vigor to the Christian church bodies of all denominations around the world was the experience of the baptism with the Holy Spirit. Millions are witnesses to the move of the Holy Spirit in bringing men and women and clergy and laity of all divisions of Christendom into groups where they find themselves one in the Spirit and one in the Lord, where real agape love for one another comes as easily as breathing, and a wholeness is shared, never before experienced since the time of the apostolic church!

The burden of this book is to explain prayerfully the experience of the baptism with the Holy Spirit, the benefits to be gained and the love and joy to be shared by all the brothers and sisters in Christ. It was prophesied in both the Old and the New Testaments and is now coming to pass in our glorious day. Millions share the common conviction, on the basis of what is happening to all Christian churches all over the world, that we are in the period of time described as "the last days," and we share with equal enthusiasm in the singing of the song that says,

> There's never been a day like this day to me!
> There's never been a day like this day I see!
> There's never been a light that shineth so
>   bright as this day, this glorious day!

And the phrase with which the early Christians greeted one another is again coming from the lips of millions of His children: "Maranatha!" (The Lord is coming!")

The intent of this book is not to be critical but rather to share with everyone who is interested the phenomenon known as the baptism with the Holy Spirit. This experience will not make you more of a Christian, but you will be a more powerful Christian and will be better able to witness to the glory of Jesus Christ both "in Jerusalem, and in all Judea, and in Samaria, and unto the uttermost part of the earth!" To this end we prayerfully offer this book.

Norris L. Wogen

12

CHAPTER 1

The summer of 1967 was a beautiful period in my ministry. St. Stephen's Lutheran Church in Cedar Rapids, Iowa, the parish I had been pastoring for fifteen years, was within thirty days of signing a contract with an architect for a new church plant. The mantle of success was beginning to rest comfortably on my shoulders, and a sense of well-being pervaded my days. I loved my God and felt loved by Him. Church membership had grown from a handful of members to the point that we had to provide three services each Sunday morning to accommodate our people. More significantly, we needed two complete Sunday schools and a Bethel Bible teacher-training program; yet despite the abruptness of our expansion, the Lord always provided teachers and staff. I was at peace and happy in my profession.

But, as is sometimes the case on an ideal summer day, storm clouds may appear on the horizon that can bring either the assurance of an abundant harvest or the end of hope for the season. In my case the storm came up so suddenly that there was no warning.

One evening a committee arrived at the door of my office. I smiled and invited them in, but there were no returning smiles as they handed me a formal-looking document that turned out to be a petition from a group within the congregation. My eyes caught the first four lines and I could go no further:

> We, the undersigned members of St. Stephen's Lutheran congregation, request the resignation of the Rev. Norris L. Wogen as Pastor of St. Stephen's Lutheran Congregation, said resignation to take effect as soon as possible.

I just stood there, blinking, unable to breathe, waiting for the roof to fall in. I forced myself to read on. There seemed to be a list of grievances—familiar to any pastor who has stuck to a strong position or locked horns with any clique in his parish. I was a dictator. I removed members from the congregation's rolls without reason or authority. I catered to people of wealth. I spent money without authorization. People were frightened by me and afraid to approach me for fear of censure.

Thus began a nightmare from which I was not to awaken for several weeks. There is nothing quite so ugly as a church fight when the gloves finally come off, perhaps because we

Christians, who have had a taste of what real righteousness is—His righteousness—have a far greater capacity for *self*-righteousness. And no one is so adamant as a Christian who knows he is right. The congregation became divided into two groups: those for and those against the removal of the pastor.

Groups of people came to the pastor's office to say that if he left, they were leaving, too. Others made it known that if he *stayed*, they were leaving. Desperate unity meetings only deepened the chasms of disunity, until finally the bishop was called in for two incredible six-hour sessions with the church council, followed by two horrendous full congregational meetings.

The bishop's decision was firm, and his statement to the congregation added a touch of hope to a seemingly hopeless situation: "I see no reason for the separation of congregation and pastor here. My advice to you is to iron out your differences and get busy building the kingdom!"

But the mingling of fact and fiction in the charges and counter-charges between the warring parts of the congregation had created wounds that defied healing. For, again, nothing is so bitter or unforgiving as a self-righteous individual who has been wronged when he *knows* he's right. That is when the issues invariably seem to be matters of life and death, for it is always agony to witness the rending asunder

of a body, especially when it is the Body of
Christ. Those destined by God to spend eternity
as brothers went separate ways; and, though the
issue was settled, there were some who persisted
in guerrilla warfare long after hostilities had
ceased, and peace was the one thing almost all
parties longed for.

It did not just end with the cease fire; the
conflict writhed and twitched on, continuing the
mental anguish on all sides. And if we human
beings suffer and feel the drain on our spirits,
who can measure the extent of Christ's agony?
Jesus wept over Jerusalem; how much more
does He weep over today? We are not alone
in our sorrow.

I began taking long walks in the sleepless
hours of the early morning, listening to my foot-
falls on the pavement and brooding about what
was happening to my church. Sometimes I put
the top down on my convertible and drove aim-
lessly through the dark from one small town
to another, the wind blowing through my hair,
my topcoat buttoned up around my neck and
the heater on high. And more than once, as a
concrete bridge abutment loomed into sight, the
thought would come into my mind that a slight
turn of the wheel would end all my problems.
But even in the depths of despair, I knew that
no agony on earth could begin to compare with
the endless hell that awaited the suicide.

There is nothing unique, of course, in suffering. Sooner or later, to a lesser or greater degree, all men walk that dark street. The president of Luther Theological Seminary had warned us of such times a quarter of a century before, "When you walk through the valley of decision, you walk alone." These are times when there are no shoulders to cry on. How I wanted to turn time back fifty years to find again the shoulder I had found comfort on as a child! But it wasn't there any more. There was only God, and while I knew Him, I didn't know Him well enough to let Him be my Comforter.

To be sure, He had blessed the parish tremendously; why, we even had three vocal choirs and a handbell choir! We were a busy people enjoying the stability and attractiveness that goes with a successful church program. The continuous adult membership courses were regularly adding new members, and finances were no problem: in order to build the new church we had voted on, we needed to increase our annual income only $440 a year.

It was to be a magnificent edifice: a stone church in Gothic style, air-conditioned, the choir in stalls near the altar instead of in the balcony, and there was even provision made for a full-scale pipe organ. Out front, a parabolic arch was to face the main thoroughfare, and a flood-lit, seventeen-foot statue of Christ would be visible for five blocks down Thirty-second Street, day or night.

Until the night the petition was tendered, it seemed to me that about all we had to do to achieve our new church plant was to keep on breathing. The numerical growth of the congregation was assured, a greater impact on the neighborhood and city was almost certain, and Christ was sure to be glorified. I wept as this dream shattered, and was sure then that Christ wept with me.

The period following the final outcome of the struggle was marked by members' decisions to go or to stay. Most of those in the opposition felt they had gone too far to turn back. Others, who really had no strong feelings themselves about the issues, were nonetheless sympathetic to the losers and left with them. Some were disillusioned by the conflict itself and sought to erase it from their minds by going elsewhere. By the time all the adjustments were made, we had lost one-third of the congregation.

No matter what the outcome on the battlefield, a soldier who has signed up for the duration has no real options. He must go on fighting. Nor is it any different in the Lord's army. You may be angry at your commanding officer, you may feel like deserting, or at least going AWOL for a season of R & R. But instead, you shoulder your weapon and return to the trenches at His call. "No man, having set his hands to the plow, and looking backwards, is worthy of the kingdom."

In those dark days, the Gethsemane prayer of Christ took on a depth of meaning for me that it had never had before, "Father, if it be thy will, let this cup pass from me. Nevertheless, not my will but thine be done." I was to remain in my pulpit, no matter how much I wanted to leave.

And so I continued to work as hard as time and health would permit. And never had I prayed more fervently. But all the prayers and all the effort brought little results, and I was faced with the spectre of myself treading water —and losing spiritual buoyancy. Futility dogged my heels and frustration became my response to practically everything.

After two years of arduous, fruitless endeavor, I became convinced that there *had* to be more to this business of pastoring than I was aware of. "If there isn't," I decided, "I am going to get out." And I meant it.

But I knew that Jesus meant it, too, in John 14:13, when He said, "Whatsoever ye shall ask in my name, that will I do, that the Father may be glorified in the Son!" So that's where I began, by asking. Actually I had been asking for some time, but I wasn't getting any real answers. Could I possibly have alienated my God to the extent that He was willing to let all our plans fail? Did it take *this* for Him to get my attention? Did I actually give Him no other choice?

I was directed to the reading of the Psalms,

and before long I became aware that one could not read more than four consecutive Psalms anywhere without coming on a refrain of a man calling out to God from the depths of despair. "Lord, hear my voice! Let thine ears be attentive to the voice of my supplications!"

Well, that's what I was doing, crying out. And then one day, in Psalm 34, I found what I was looking for. "The righteous cry, and the Lord heareth, and delivereth them out of all their troubles . . . out of them all . . . the Lord redeemeth the soul of his servants: and none of them that trust in him shall be desolate."

God *was* in charge, no matter what happened, or how far away He seemed. For the matter wasn't with Him; it was with me. If I was desolate, that was my own doing and my own lack of trust. So God could use even seeming disaster to reach us and work new life in us. And Romans 8:28 became a tremendous promise, "We know that all things work together for good to them that love God, to them who are the called according to his purpose."

I was called—that much I knew. And my faith was built up immeasurably by the assurance that indeed God *was* working out His purpose in my life. Had He permitted me to reach a new low in my life in order that He might raise me up? I prayed that it might be so.

Gradually, painfully I began to understand. Had we succeeded in building our church, had

the congregation continued to flourish, we would
have wound up prosperous, successful—and
dead. Beauty, bigness and prestige had been
our goals—my goals—but I was coming to realize that the most important things in the world
are not the building of an imposing edifice and
the maintenance of a large congregation. Getting close to God, and staying there, were.

Clearly He did not want all the trappings
of worldly success. But what *did* He want?

CHAPTER 2

How did a Lutheran pastor with twenty-six years in the ministry start to enlarge his theological "inventory"? *Carefully*. The Lutheran theological format was about as inflexible as it was possible to be. For over four hundred years the statement of Martin Luther's that never failed to strike a responsive chord had been: "Here I stand! God help me! I cannot do otherwise!"

The Lutheran knowledge of God was a sure one. Men had bled and died for it. Some of the greatest theologians of history had worked unstintingly over our doctrines, and these had proved adequate to bring heathen into a living relationship with the Triune God. Cathedrals had been erected by people of this faith, and they still stood today as lofty sentinels, pointing man Godward. For centuries there had been staunch witnesses to this faith. The Reformation hymn "A Mighty Fortress Is Our God" had been and was being sung by millions of faithful adherents to our doctrines. Could anyone dare suggest that something new might be added?

There were three guiding principles to which all Lutherans pointed with pride: The *Word Alone*, signifying the fact that in the Lutheran church we taught only what we could prove by Scripture. *Grace Alone*, which meant that salvation was a gift from God: you couldn't buy it, earn it or suffer for it—it was a gift. And *Faith Alone*, which was the hand that accepted the gift of salvation. "He that believeth on Me, though he were dead, yet shall he live!"

Much of the strength of the Lutheran church derived from its intensive educational program for its members. There was a minimum of two years of in-depth training of the young in preparation for confirmation. When they stood before the altar of God to answer the questions: "Do you believe in God the Father Almighty, Maker of heaven and earth? Do you believe in Jesus Christ, His only begotten Son, our Lord? Do you believe in the Holy Spirit, the Holy Christian Church?", for the vast majority there was a solemnity and meaning to this experience that remained throughout life.

In an effort to maintain Christian education through college and university training, the church provided a number of major seats of learning across the nation, from Wagner College in New York to Pacific Lutheran College on the

West Coast. Lutheran Christians are respected around the world. Was it reasonable to assume that there could be something more than was there in the teachings of this church?

I found myself caught on the horns of a dilemma: there had to be something more than I was using. Yet how could there be?

In 1969 my search finally took me outside familiar Lutheran territory, to the United States Congress on Evangelism in Minneapolis, Minnesota. Dr. Billy Graham was the honorary chairman, Dr. Oswald Hoffman of the Lutheran Hour was the acting chairman, Dr. Leighton Ford, Billy Graham's brother-in-law, was one of the speakers, and Pastor Tom Skinner, the black former leader of one of the most feared gangs in New York City, was another. Seven thousand people gathered there. The delegates came from all fifty states of the Union and eleven different countries, and ninety-three different denominations were represented.

It was a different kind of meeting for a staid conservative Lutheran. "Praise the Lord!" interrupted the speeches, and the many "Amens" didn't signify the end of anything, merely agreement. And once I was startled by a loud "Hallelujah!" But all the exuberant distraction did not prevent the message from coming through. And here was the first hint that Lutherans did not have everything that might be used to promote the kingdom. At the very least, I and the other Lutherans present faced the fact that God had some children who were not Lutherans!

I discovered that there are substantial benefits to be gained from mingling with others in God's household. Pastor Tom Skinner spoke with a conviction—and sometimes a fury—that had a tremendous impact. A hush fell over the audience as he made us realize some of the sins we had committed against other races, and we were ashamed. We had paid lip-service, but never really sought or worked for solutions. At this meeting we were humbled, repentant, and moved to become more reasonable.

There were a number of similar albeit smaller meetings in the ensuing months, as my horizons continued to be expanded, and I came to realize that there was a sizable body of committed ministers of all denominations, eager to fellowship and support one another "in the faith." I began to realize that what the Bible said about the early Apostolic church was happening again.

Then during the summer and fall of '69 came the sequence of events which, as it had for so many other seekers, really shifted my search into high gear. A book came into my hands that stirred me more deeply than any I had read other than the Bible. It was the story of a rural preacher who learned to walk by faith and be led almost totally by the Holy Spirit, and who God was then able to use to perform miracles

in the ghettos of Brooklyn equal to the Acts of
the Apostles—*The Cross and the Switchblade.*

I got so excited when I read that book, I
could hardly sit still to finish it. Impulsively
I called David Wilkerson in his Teen Challenge
office. "I've just finished your book," I blurted
out. "I want to talk to you!"

"What do you want to talk to me about?"
he said.

"About the baptism with the Holy Spirit,"
I told him, "and about this speaking-in-tongues
business."

"Do you ever get to New York?" he asked.

"I can be there tomorrow," I said impulsively, and without further delay I boarded a plane
in Cedar Rapids at 7:30 the next morning and
at 2:05 I walked into the Teen Challenge Center
in Brooklyn.

The Lord is truly merciful to those who ear-
nestly seek Him, and He gives us beginners a
long leash. I was taken on a tour of the place,
and I saw the realities which had already become so real in the book. As it turned out, I
spent most of my time there with Susie Vasques,
one of the main characters of another book Dave
had written, *Twelve Angels from Hell.* Susie had
been on heroin for twelve years, and a prostitute
for all that time to support herself in her ex-
pensive habit. She showed me where she had
injected dope. They looked as though they had

been peppered with shotgun pellets. As she spoke of her faith and the love she now had for the Lord, she said softly, "Oh, if it wasn't for Jesus, I would be dead!"

Susie was as lovely a lady as I have ever met. God had reached down into the hell of the dope addict's world and lifted Susie out of her misery and put her on a glory road. And the mute witness of her changed life was as eloquent as any evangelistic message I had heard. And there was something more—a desire to be led by the Holy Spirit in everything, the little things as well as the big. This had been the element which had struck the deepest chord in me as I had read the book, and now I had seen with my own eyes the fruit of a Spirit-filled, Spirit-*led* life. And I knew that this was what I had been looking for, for so long. The one-day trip to New York was another step completed in my search.

As soon as I reached home, I went to the first Pentecostal pastor I could find, saying, "You've got something I want. Will you tell me about the baptism with the Holy Spirit and pray for me that I may receive it?" He was most kind and tried to explain it to me and prayed for me, but nothing happened. I went to another and another with still no success, until I began to wonder if there were something terribly wrong with me. "Have I offended God in some way that He is not going to permit me to know the joy and the peace and the love and the power these others know?''

I went to Pentecostal service after service, seeking the experience I knew I needed to live the life I was called to. I heard people speaking in tongues all around me and usually in a barely audible whisper. I saw and heard things never witnessed in a Lutheran church. But always I was an observer—never a participant.

"Why not me, Lord?" I prayed by myself; I prayed with members of the congregations. I prayed in my own church and in my office, and everywhere I seemed to meet only silence. It was as if God was somehow testing the depth of my commitment. I knew I was on the right track, for we have a command to be filled and led by the Holy Spirit. Ephesians 5:18 tells us, "Don't drink too much wine, for many evils lie along that path; be filled instead with the Holy Spirit, and controlled by Him." But nothing I did, and no one I saw seemed to be able to help.

For almost a year futility dogged my search, until in January, 1970, I was scheduled to go to Fort Lauderdale, Florida, to attend an evangelism clinic in the Coral Ridge Presbyterian Church under the leadership of Dr. James Kennedy. "All right, Lord, this is it! I am going to go to Fort Lauderdale three days early and find a Pentecostal pastor and if necessary camp on his doorstep the whole three days, but I am determined to receive the baptism with the Holy Spirit. It's now or never!"

Of course I did not hear any answer: in those days I was not very good at hearing Him if He thundered, let alone spoke in a still, small voice in the heart. But looking back, I can imagine He must have smiled at my ultimatum.

My plane arrived in Fort Lauderdale Wednesday noon, the 28th of January. I was soon settled in the private home where I was to be a guest for the week. Thursday morning I rented a car and carried on my search. By now the whole thing was in God's hands, though of course I thought I was doing it all myself. It occurred to me to look in the yellow pages for Pentecostal churches, and I found two listed. The first I noticed was called "Pentecostal Holiness"—and that, for a Lutheran, was simply too frightening.

The other was called "Faith Farm Mission." Well, now, this was more like it. "Faith"—we talked about that all the time in the Lutheran church. "Farm"—I grew up on one. And "Mission"—I was familiar with mission endeavors. It would be smaller, less imposing, more comfortable. There was no question about it, this was the church for me! And as eager as I was to get there and get on with it, I felt a strange peace settle over me, almost as if I were riding in the car instead of driving it.

Fort Lauderdale is a city of canals, the Venice of the United States. However, there weren't quite enough bridges, so locating the Mission wasn't easy. Eventually I found myself bouncing along an impossibly narrow, two-track lane, increasingly dubious over the whole adventure. I had not traveled far before I came to several huge piles of junk on both sides of the lane. There were old sinks, bathtubs, window sashes, cars, furniture—every imaginable kind of junk.

What on earth was I doing there anyway? I wondered.

I must have been out of my mind! And I determined that the first time there was enough room to turn around, I would do just that and wash my hands of the whole absurd notion . . . only there was no place to turn around.

Abruptly, on the other side of a small hill of debris, some office buildings came into view —and a lovely chapel with palm trees around it. Well, of all the unlikely—

I parked my car and headed for the chapel, looking for a minister, but finding none. I sat down in a pew, now acutely self-conscious and wishing I were a thousand miles away—or about thirteen hundred and twenty-five, to be more exact. At that moment a man who may have been the handyman came in, and I asked him if there was a minister available.

"Oh, yes," he said, "we have four of them."

"Four!" I exclaimed. "*Here*?" Then immediately regretting my rudeness, I hurried on. "I would like to talk to one of them. Which one would you recommend?" He frowned and shook his head. "Oh, I'm no respecter of persons!"

"That's wonderful," I managed to say, beginning to wonder if I hadn't stepped through Alice's looking glass. "But if you had a problem, which one of them would you go to?"

"Well," he said, stopping to rub his nose and inspect some lint on the sleeve of his shirt. "I'm no respecter of persons, mind you, but—I suppose—I would go see Joe Bates."

"That is the one *I* want to see," I declared.

"Follow me," he said abruptly, and without waiting for a reply he turned and led the way to Reverend Bates' office.

I had made up my mind at the outset of this search for the baptism that I was going to be myself—a Lutheran to the core—not ready to accept just any theological package that came along for the sake of receiving the baptism. So that was how I stated my case. "I am interested in the baptism with the Holy Spirit, but as far as this speaking-in-tongues business is concerned, I couldn't care less!"

How patient and kind and longsuffering our God is! His humble and obedient servant, Joe Bates, acted as if he hadn't heard a word. He shared with me at length, and I with him, and after an hour or so, he said, "You know, Brother

Wogen, you really ought to see Brother Garland. He's the one who runs this place. He will be a great blessing to you."

"This place" was an alcoholics' rehabilitation center, as well as a congregational worship center, and Brother Garland Eastham was the founder and president of Faith Farm Mission. For many years he was a member of a Missouri Synod Lutheran congregation in Ohio and a very active deacon. About twenty-six years ago he received the baptism with the Holy Spirit, and because of this, he was no longer wanted as a member of that congregation. Not long afterward, God called him to the mission he is involved in at Fort Lauderdale: working with alcoholics. And despite the unassuming physical plant, God has blessed his ministry abundantly, freeing countless numbers from alcohol enslavement and leading them into His kingdom.

When Joe Bates and I found his director, I was somewhat disappointed. I had imagined I was going to meet some sort of giant. Instead, here was a rather short, quite unexceptional looking man. How deceiving looks are, and how foolish we are to make snap judgments!

We had spoken only briefly when Garland said, "The Lord sent you here. He sends a lot of ministers and priests here for the same reason you came."

I just shook my head in wonder. And I began to appreciate the wisdom of God in leading me to this man. In His time, and in His way, He had brought me to Garland Eastham.

Garland was still very much a Lutheran in his theology, and as such he was able to lead me step by step through the Scriptures, making it clear to me that the charismatic renewal being experienced in every so-called mainline church in the world today was prophesied in both the Old and New Testaments. In its purest form it is completely in line with Scripture.

As Garland patiently explained it, the Holy Spirit has been and is a vital part of the whole divine plan for the earth's creation. His first efforts are recorded in the first chapter of Genesis, the second verse, "And the Spirit of God moved upon the face of the waters." The outpouring of the Holy Spirit was promised way back in Isaiah 32:15, "Until the spirit be poured upon us from on high, and the wilderness be a fruitful field." Also in Isaiah 59:21, "As for me, this is my covenant with them, saith the Lord; My Spirit that is upon thee, and my words which I have put in thy mouth, shall not depart out of thy mouth, nor out of the mouth of thy seed, nor out of the mouth of thy seed's seed, saith the Lord, from henceforth and for ever." (That obviously includes today.) In Zechariah 4:6, "Then he answered and spake unto me, saying, This is the word of the Lord unto Zerubbabel, saying, Not by might, nor by power, but by my spirit, saith the Lord of hosts."

In Ezekiel 36:27, God speaks further of the indwelling of the Holy Spirit, "And I will put my spirit within you, and cause you to walk in my statutes, and ye shall keep my judgments and do them." And again in Ezekiel 39:29, "Neither will I hide my face any more from them: for I have poured out my spirit upon the house of Israel, saith the Lord God."

Then there is the prophecy most often referred to today, from Joel 2:28, "And it shall come to pass afterward, that I will pour out my spirit upon all flesh; and your sons and your daughters shall prophesy, your old men shall dream dreams, your young men shall see visions."

As Garland knitted together these references to the Holy Spirit, I began to understand the third part of the Trinity for the first time in the light of Scripture and to sense His role in God's scheme of things as never before. For instance, I was astonished at how many men (and not just prophets, either) were filled with the Spirit in the Old Testament: the elders in Numbers 11:25, Balaam in Numbers 24:2, Othniel in Judges 3:10, Gideon in Judges 6:34, Samson in Judges 14:6, Saul in 1 Samuel 10:10, David in 1 Samuel 16:13.

But it was in the New Testament, of course, that God's plan for us regarding the Holy Spirit really came clear. I had read the pertinent scriptures many times in the course of my regular

Bible study, but never had they been taken in sequence and illuminated by the Spirit himself, through His obvious inspired spokesman, Garland.

To begin with, I saw that in each of the Gospels, John the Baptist made it quite clear that, while he was baptizing with water, He who came after him would baptize with the Holy Spirit (Matt. 3:11, Mark 1:8, Luke 3:16, John 1:33). So Jesus himself did the baptizing . . . and when He spoke of those who believed in Him having rivers of living water flowing from within them (John 7:38, 39), John made the point that Jesus was referring to the Holy Spirit, which His believers would receive after He had gone to be with His Father—just as He assured the twelve at the Last Supper (John 14:16-17, 16:7) when He tried to cheer them with the promise of another Comforter whom He would send to take His place.

Until they received the Holy Spirit themselves, of course, there was no way that the disciples could know what Jesus was talking about, but it was abundantly clear that He put a higher value on this gift than on anything else (Luke 11:11-13). In fact, the last thing He told them before ascending to be with His Father was that they should stay in Jerusalem until He sent the power from on high (Luke 24:49), reminding them that while John (the Baptist) baptized with water, they would soon be baptized with the Holy Ghost and receive the power

He spoke of (Acts 1:5, 8). This power would enable them to witness to the ends of the earth, not just with their lips but *in their lives*; in other words, power that would enable them to live overcoming lives that would be the strongest witness of all.

They did exactly as He instructed, and sure enough, ten days later, on the ancient harvest festival day, 120 of them were suddenly filled with the Holy Spirit (Acts 2:4). Peter certainly had new power: 3,000 were converted at the first sermon he preached. And in that sermon, by way of explanation of the fantastic thing that had happened to them, he quoted the prophecy of Joel, "And it shall come to pass in the last days, saith God, I will pour out of my spirit upon all flesh" (Acts 2:17ff.). And he closed by calling on all of them to first repent, then be baptzied in the name of Jesus, and then they would receive the gift of the Holy Spirit (Acts 2:38).

Not long after that, word came that somebody (Philip) was busy converting the Samaritans, of all people; and the apostles sent two of their number, Peter and John, to check out what was going on. The report was true, but when Peter and John saw that the conversion had not included the receiving of the Holy Spirit, they prayed and laid their hands on the Samaritan believers, and they were filled with the Spirit (Acts 8:14-17).

Six years later, Paul was converted on the

road to Damascus. Shortly after his blinding conversion, he was visited by Ananias who, laying his hands on Paul's head, told him that the Lord Jesus had sent him that he might receive his sight and be filled with the Holy Spirit. And he did (Acts 9:17, 18). Not long after, at the house of Cornelius in Caesarea, a roomful of Gentiles were filled with the Spirit just listening to Peter preach (Acts 10:44, 45), recalling which, Peter remembered the words of Jesus when He said, "You'll be baptized with the Holy Spirit" (Acts 11:15, 16).

The fifth and last New Testament account of the baptism with the Holy Spirit occurred some thirty years later when Paul discovered some Ephesian believers who, when asked if they had received the Holy Spirit, said that they'd never heard of Him. Paul quickly remedied that—first baptizing them in the name of Jesus and then laying on hands for them to receive the infilling of the Holy Spirit, which they did (Acts 19:2-7).

It was quite a tour Garland took me on, at the end of which he pointed out that nowhere in any of the scriptures had he found one verse which said that this pattern was not to be continued today. Comforter, teacher, enabler—the Holy Spirit was the vehicle by which "the love of God is shed abroad in our hearts" (Rom. 5:5), a most precious gift which we were specifically charged by Paul to be filled with (Eph.

5:18) and which we were on no account to neglect (I Tim. 4:14).

Garland and I sat and talked for three hours until my mind felt as if it could absorb no more; and my heart, as happy as it was, was exhausted. Then he invited me to join him and the men of the Mission for lunch, and I did.

After sensing that I needed a chance to assimilate all the information I had been given, he suggested that we not meet again until 7:30 that evening. I was grateful: I had already spent three hours in conversation with him and one hour with Joe Bates. I was talked—and listened —out. I spent the afternoon driving and resting, and that, too, was in God's plan, for when I returned, our discussion resumed and continued far into the night.

Finally, at 12:30 in the early morning, I ran out of questions. To what must have been Garland's heartfelt relief, though he never showed anything but the most incredible patience. In eight hours, despite some pretty provocative, even belligerent questions, he never once indicated anything but the kindest and yet perceptive consideration. Which was itself a persuasive witness to the power that came with a Spirit-filled, Spirit-led walk.

There was a silence, and then he said, "Pastor Wogen, let us pray!" I knelt on the floor facing the side of a metal folding chair, with my elbows in the seat of the chair and my hands folded. Garland placed one hand on my head; the other was raised in a supplicating gesture heavenward. He was alternately praying in tongues and in English. Suddenly I collapsed on the chair as though I had been poleaxed, though there was no pain, other than a tingling sensation, involved. One arm went through the back of the chair, the other across the front, with my chest resting on the seat of the chair and my head hanging limp over the other side. Garland's prayer never ceased, but now he had his hand under my head, supporting it, instead of on top of it.

That scene remains the most vivid of any I have ever recalled, because during the time my body was on that chair, I seemed to be looking down on it from above, or over at it from alongside. I saw the whole thing as a bystander, and I understood many things in those moments, of the difference between body and soul—a difference I had heretofore minimized. And then I understood the terrible importance of salvation and going God's way here on earth. For it determined how our immortal soul would spend the rest of eternity. For all its exhilaration—and I heard everything that was being said and could move about the room whenever I wished, unencumbered by the force of gravity, let alone my inert body—it was—and remains—a profoundly sobering experience.

I had no awareness of the passage of time;

it just seemed that after awhile I was back in my body again, and I broke out in a burst of laughter. It was unusual, but not hysterical, laughter and it seemed to come from deeper inside of me than any laughter ever had before. And the more it came, the more joy I felt. And love for God. And praise.

I got back on my knees and raised both hands in the air. As I did so, it felt as if I had put all ten fingers in electric light sockets. Something like electricity seemed to flow down through my fingers, arms and body and down to my feet. In a very short time, I who had said, "As far as tongues is concerned, I couldn't care less," began praising God in a language that I didn't recognize, and which seemed to come straight from my heart, as if my heart had been given its own voice and could tell God directly how much it loved Him. I had judged in ignorance when I had spoken against tongues, and I praise God that He does not hold our ignorance against us! For years I had spoken against and ridiculed these "holy rollers." But the Lord forgives. I had asked for power—power to enable me to really *live* the life He had called me to, to *be* the disciple that He wanted me to be that my life itself might be a witness to the glory of God, even more than any words I might speak. That takes the empowering of the Holy Spirit, and that is what we receive when we ask Jesus to baptize us in the Holy Spirit.

Sometimes we are "slain" in the spirit, as I was; sometimes we speak in tongues; and sometimes the infilling is a quiet, gradual deepening, but the joy that floods the soul cannot be described. It is but a foretaste of the kingdom of God, and while it does modulate with time and growth, we are never the same again.

Somehow, by the grace of God, I found my way back to the place I was staying that night, praising God all the way and grinning like a kid on Christmas morning. I didn't think I would sleep at all, but I slept as if I'd been drugged, so completely wrung out was I.

And the next morning, Satan was ready with his bucket of cold water in the face, just like he always is. I began to doubt my experience. I went back to see Garland and immediately asked him, "Did I really speak in tongues last night?" "I'll say you did," he laughed, and then became suddenly serious, "After you left, the Lord gave me two things concerning you. First, you are going to be used as an apostle to bring the charismatic renewal to the Lutherans."

This was too much! I, who recently had just had one-third of my congregation leave our church in protest to my pastorship, who was probably last and least among the five thousand pastors or more in the American Lutheran Church, I was going to be an apostle to the Lutherans? Not very likely! My mind said, "This is an old man. Humor him but forget it. Don't make a fool of yourself."

If Garland sensed my skepticism, he made no indication of it. "The second thing the Lord has given me concerning you is this: He told me to call to your attention the forty-third chapter of Isaiah. You are to read it and read it, and, if possible, memorize it and never forget it. Beginning with the first verse: 'But now the Lord who created you, O Israel, says, Don't be afraid, for I have redeemed you; I have called you by name; you are mine. When you go through rivers of difficulty, you will not drown. When you walk through the fire of oppression, you will not be burned up; the flames will not consume you, for I am the Lord your God, your Savior, the Holy One of Israel.' "

That was how we parted more than four years ago, and I have never known fear since that time.

I have since thought much over what happened in Fort Lauderdale and all the things that led up to it. And I can see now the shadow of God's hand on my earlier life in ways I never dreamed of. For instance, if the church split had not happened, I might never have been motivated into an all-out search for a deeper faith. I can also see that the search was not

nearly as haphazard as it seemed, and the greatest miracle of all was His timing. To anyone
else embarking on the same search, I can verify
the truth of the passage that says, "If with
all your heart ye truly seek me, ye shall ever
surely find me."

CHAPTER 3

The shadow of His hand . . . when does a man's life begin? How much of it is of divine design? These things are often debated today by liberal theologians, mainly trying to avoid the absolute accountability and obedience implicit in Scripture. But the book of Jeremiah is certainly unequivocal, "Before I formed thee in the belly, I knew thee; and before thou camest forth out of the womb I sanctified thee, and I ordained thee a prophet unto the nations" (Jer. 1:5). And David's place in history was known long before he was born. Paul became conscious of God's plan for him, and later he was to say with a thankful heart, "I was not disobedient unto the heavenly vision!"

But Paul also knew the folly of attempting to take any credit for himself. "What do we have that we did not receive?" By surrender and obedience to God and the Lord Jesus Christ any man can say, "I live, yet not I, but Christ liveth in me; and the life which I now live in the flesh, I live by the faith of the Son of God, who loved me, and gave himself for me."

God is still doing things in the lives of His faithful people. In the history of men, though their actions and reactions are often far from His perfect will for them, nothing ever happens by happenstance. And this was one of the first things the Lord showed me as I thought about my early life and the path that had led to the baptism with the Holy Spirit and a new life of service.

I was born in 1912, the twelfth child in a family of thirteen—a family whose parents were so devout that the children never knew what it was like to be outside of the Kingdom of God. I was prayed over twice a day in my father's house while my mother was still carrying me, and this continued until I left home and, in fact, as long as my parents lived.

Every morning after breakfast, my father would read a chapter from the Bible, offer a prayer, then the family would join in the Lord's Prayer. Nor was anything ever to interrupt these devotions. If the wind-up phone rang, it was ignored, and a guest at the door would be invited in by one detailed to do so and asked to take a seat until we had finished. In the evening, Mother would conduct the devotions the same way.

In between times we were constantly busy.

Our farm may not have been the biggest in Humboldt, Iowa, but we thought it was the best, and we worked hard to keep it that way. My father fed a lot of cattle and hogs, and we raised the corn and oats to feed them. Putting up hay, shocking oats, plowing, feeding the livestock and milking some twenty dairy cows kept us moving.

On Sundays the family went to church services and Sunday school—every Sunday and every member! Some of the most violent scenes that I remember took place when some one of us decided that he was not going to church. Wielding her broom, Mother would deal in no uncertain terms with such rebellion. When she was through, peace and serenity descended on the house, and in a short time the family—the whole family—proceeded out of the house in our Sunday clothes to the buggy, wagon, sleigh, or Model T, for the ride to the church. When I was grown and long gone from home, I never received a letter from Mother that did not close with the prayer, "May God bless you to many souls' salvation."

Is there such a thing as happenstance? Proverbs 22:6 says, "Train up a child in the way he should go, and when he is old, he will not depart from it." I can speak only for my own life, but in it that has proven a divine guarantee.

My call to go into the ministry came in 1925 when I was thirteen—confirmation age. I was walking down the lane to the pasture to fetch the cows for milking, when all at once up in the sky I saw Christ in glory standing at the top of a huge golden stairway stretching into the heavens with a sort of honor guard of angels on either side flying up and down. I blinked and could hardly believe my eyes.

In my heart I knew without really understanding that God was permitting me to see something not usually given men to see. For some time, even at that age, I had prayed that God would make me a minister, and I wondered at the time if this might be His promise that one day He would.

I never shared my vision with any members of the family or anyone else, not even our pastor, whom I admired. I had been laughed at too often for sharing my thoughts and dreams with my older brothers and sisters and was not about to put such a thing into jeopardy.

The ministry was always in the back of my mind as I grew up, even though I had worked my way up in the oil business to where I was a "B" station salesman with fifteen agents to supervise—not bad for a kid of 26 back in 1938! More important, I'd been married for a year to a lovely schoolteacher named Merna Tipton, who, when I told her of my decision to ask for a transfer to running a tankwagon in order to make enough money to go to St. Olaf College to prepare for the ministry, simply said, "If you're going back to school next year anyway, why don't you quit and go back right now? I can help, and together we'll make it." And we did.

That was typical of my wife, who has been a constant support to me (and not a bad piano accompanist, either!). How grateful I am that God left nothing to chance when He set about bringing Merna and me together! In fact, He had my parents pick her out before I grew old enough or traveled far enough to make a mistake.

It happened while I was still living with my parents and working in the oil business. One day when I came home from work, both parents looked very much like a couple of cats that had just shared a canary. Mother spoke first. "We have found the girl that you should go with," she said, smiling as if it had already been settled. My thought was, this should really be something to see! Finding her had apparently begun when Mother arranged to have a neighbor take a birthday cake to my younger brother, then attending Iowa State College. When the neighbor's plans were changed, she asked a young woman friend to deliver the birthday cake. The girl agreed and came to the house to arrange the details. That's when my parents met—and chose—my wife.

I happened to be at home when she came back to pick up the cake, and I carried it out

to the car for her. She wasn't bad looking—not
at all, in fact. And with the parents so far along
in their plans for my life, the least I could
do would be to take her out. She accepted the
invitation, and not long after also accepted my
proposal of marriage.

After thirty-seven years of happiness, two
children and one grandchild to date, I'm convinced that that old custom of parents choosing
their children's mates has much to recommend
it!

My years at Luther Theological Seminary
in St. Paul, Minnesota, in the late thirties and
early forties were precious to me in many ways.
It was the "West Point" of the Lutheran church,
and we had battle-scarred veterans from the
front lines giving us practical as well as ideo-
logical advice and doctrinal training. Paul
writes to Timothy that it is vital for him to
"study to show [himself] approved unto God, a
workman that needeth not to be ashamed," and
that was pretty much our attitude at seminary:
we were being trained to be soldiers of the Lord,
with the result that we applied ourselves to the
maximum, and got a commensurate amount out
of the seminary experience.

A part of my training (though at first I did
not recognize it as such) was the summer I
spent working in the Alaskan fishing industry
during seminary. The Psalmist writes truly
when he says, "They that go down to the sea

in ships see the wonders of God in the deep."

The vastness of the sea with its many wonders and mysteries, and the smallness of man as he bounces cork-like on its surface, has a deflating effect on the ego. The seemingly endless variety, shapes, and habits of fish make us marvel at the painstaking creations of our God, and we can say "Amen!" to the eighth Psalm praising the glory of God's creative work and concluding, "O Lord, our Lord, how excellent is thy name in all the earth!"

CHAPTER 4

No one should imagine that the transition from an old way of living to a new one is easy, and this is especially true of a pastor, who has the responsibility for the spiritual well-being of his people. How would the people back at St. Stephen's react to my having received the baptism with the Holy Spirit and the gift of tongues? The mere thought of telling them appalled me. Besides, Garland Easthan had cautioned me against coming on too strong. Newly Spirit-filled pastors had been known to alienate their congregations that way, some even losing them. I came back to my parish in Cedar Rapids determined to cause no division in the congregation.

I carried on my ministry for six weeks without sharing my experience (except with Merna, of course, who accepted the change in me happily, though she didn't fully understand it—until it happened to her, too, two years later). And then one day, I called Garland. Almost his first question was, "How did your congregation take your experience?"

"I haven't told them yet."

"You haven't told them yet?" he repeated, surprised.

"You've got to tell them."

"But, you told me I had to be careful," I countered.

"Careful, yes, but not deceptive. You've got to declare the whole counsel of God. Don't worry; the Holy Spirit will show you how and when and will prepare their hearts. He'll even give you the words."

As Garland spoke, I sensed it was the Lord himself speaking through him, and already I knew the time and the place. "I will tell them Sunday morning, in the adult class."

Although I had told no one about my experience, it was nonetheless obvious that my ministry had changed. More members were attending service regularly than ever before, and the number in my Sunday morning Bible class had tripled in the six weeks since my return. These trusting souls were about to become the first recipients of my bombshell.

Sunday morning arrived, and I announced to the class that instead of our regular lesson I was going to take the whole hour to share with them my Florida experience. And I did, leaving out nothing. They sat more or less open-mouthed throughout, and at the conclusion of the hour, I asked if they had noticed any difference in me since my return.

All of them said they knew something must have happened to me, but they didn't know what. They said that the Bible class had become stimulating and that accounted for the increased attendance. Also, my preaching had improved, they said, and they didn't want to miss a single service.

Christianity was becoming exciting to them! They had tasted and found it a delightful experience. To myself I praised the Lord for giving me the right words, and for the patience He gave me to wait those six weeks before I told them. They had learned to love the things of the Spirit before they knew these came by way of the baptism with the Holy Spirit! For me that was especially rewarding.

No one needs to wave a banner indicating that he has been filled with the Spirit. If you really have been filled with the Spirit, you begin to *live* your Christianity. It is no longer the assignment of a new life pattern, it is the sudden blossoming of a spiritual springtime in your heart. You actually love people! Forgiving is no problem, even the most grievous wrong. It was no idle promise when Jesus said, "You shall receive power after the Holy Spirit has come upon you, and you shall be my witnesses." And what a difference the baptism with the Holy Spirit makes in your witness as a Christian personality! You are eager to evidence your allegiance to the King of kings, and it comes almost as naturally as breathing. Another spark had alighted, another tiny fire had been kindled. It was not long before others in our congregation sought and received the infilling of the Spirit and likewise became effective witnesses of the Spirit's power to renew. Soon we had evening prayer groups meeting in the parsonage and on the patio in the backyard. The study in the parsonage became the main prayer room where several received the baptism. People came to these informal prayer groups from many other Protestant churches and from the Catholic church; in fact, a number of sisters received the baptism.

One of the beautiful things, we discovered immediately, was the oneness of the Body of Christ! You love one another in Christ, regardless of church, sect or denomination. You are brothers and sisters in Christ, and there is no end to this relationship. Almost everything else will pass away, Scripture tells us, including the gift of "tongues," but love will never die. Our wondrous love for one another will never dim, only intensify.

As part of our evangelistic effort, we started prayer meetings in the church Thursday mornings at five o'clock and prayed for two hours on our knees. The chairs were arranged in a circle and each knelt in front of his or her chair, putting elbows in the seat of the chair. We took turns praying around the circle randomly as the Spirit led, each one participating or not as he wished. Each provided his own pillow for those two hours of kneeling in prayer, and no one forgot his pillow more than once!

One of the gifts of the Spirit that I particularly sought was the gift of healing. I had lived through the days when some prominent theologians were promoting the idea that "God is dead," and it seemed to me that the most emphatic refutation of that position was contained in contemporary cases of divine healing. I wanted as many as possible to see that God was very much alive, so I prayed for that gift.

And so it was that at one of our Thursday morning meetings, I prayed for one of the regulars who that morning was not there, "God, please take the pain out of Polly's joints." No sooner had the words come out of my mouth than I realized that was a pretty clumsy way to pray. Normally I might have prayed, "God, please heal Polly of her arthritis." It is not unusual for a pastor to criticize himself, but when you have spoken aloud, it has to stand.

Later that same morning one of the members of the congregation called and asked if I would mind picking up Polly and taking her to the neighboring town of Marion. The caller had heard I was going there anyway so thought I wouldn't mind having a passenger. I said, fine, and that I was glad she was all right, as we'd missed her at the prayer meeting.

When I stopped at Polly's home, I asked as usual, "How are things going with you today, Polly? How do you feel?"

I will never forget her reply. "I feel wonderful!" she replied. "The pain went out of my joints this morning!"

"What did you say?"

"I said, the pain went out of my joints this morning!"

Shivers went up and down my spine as I realized that Jesus had answered my prayer—verbatim! God would and did "heal in the name Jesus!" Since then I have seen hundreds, if not thousands, of healings of a great variety of ills, but this first one gave me the greatest thrill.

For anyone who has witnessed such a healing, it is no longer a question of theological debate. Jesus is the healer today, even as He was two thousand years ago. What's more, He says in John 14:12, "He that believeth on me, the works that I do shall he do also; and greater works than these shall he do; because I go unto my Father." Just think of the things Jesus did: He healed all kinds of diseases; the lame walked; the blind saw; the deaf heard. He stilled the storms; He drove out demons; He raised the dead. And there are reliable reports of these things being done in this day and age in various parts of the world.

Many Charismatics today are in much the same position to witness for Christ as was the Apostle John when he wrote that first letter, "That which was from the beginning, which we have heard, which we have seen with our eyes, which we have looked upon and our hands have handled, of the word of life, declare we unto thee." In the name of Jesus, all things are possible. This is the potential of the Spirit walk!

The word began to spread. One Sunday afternoon, Reba and Vern, friends from a neighboring town, called and said, "We would like to come and talk with you." They wanted to know about the baptism. After we had spent a couple of hours discussing the experience, I simply asked, "Look, would you like to have prayer for the baptism?"

"Yes, if you aren't too busy," they answered almost together.

"Do you mind if I call some of the Catholic sisters and have them pray with me?"

They approved. (When a Lutheran couple readily agree to have Catholic sisters pray for them, you may be sure they are ready for the baptism!) Three of the sisters came and all of us knelt on the carpet in the study, alternately praying and singing.

After some time I thought that maybe we had better stop. It didn't look as if anything was going to happen. Then Sister Ann demonstrated the gift that women apparently have from birth—they can see around corners. "Let's not stop now," she urged, as if she had read my mind. "The Spirit is here; wait just a few moments."

Her prediction was correct. In just a few moments both Reba and Vern began sobbing softly, and after a few more seconds, went into laughter. Theirs was no hysteria, just boundless joy in the Lord! In the midst of her laughter, Reba reached out, and, touching her husband on the shoulder, said, "See! I told you it was real, Vern!"

No one can know how real or how delightful it is to receive the baptism with the Holy Spirit until it is experienced. For Vern and Reba this has given them a new way of life, a new joy and a zest for living they never knew before. Both of them have experienced healings as the result of prayer, and several others have been led into the Spirit walk by them.

My wife and I have had several reasons to praise the Lord in our daily lives. One morning she complained of intense pain in her teeth. I thought little about it, because my wife often drinks extremely hot coffee, and when she would take a drink of very cold water immediately afterwards, it seems likely that could cause the pain. But the next morning she complained again of the same intense pain in her jaws, so, after our devotions, I put my hands on her jaws and prayed for healing. The pain left her and never troubled her again.

Not long after, her sciatic nerve was strained because of a long automobile trip to northern Michigan. The doctor had told her there was not much that could be done but to give her leg as much rest as possible. One night she was tossing and turning in bed with pain and asked me to pray for her leg. The next morning she thanked me for the prayer. "It helped a great deal. I went to sleep and slept the rest of the night."

There have been times when I have been in the presence of cripples or parents with crippled children, and I have wondered if they would like to be prayed for. All cripples want to be healed, but not all cripples have faith, and Hebrews 11:6 states simply, "He that cometh to God must believe that he is, and that he is a rewarder of them that diligently seek him."

You don't walk up to a man walking with a limp and ask him, "How would you like to walk on two good legs?" He will be looking to you, instead of God, and it is unlikely that much will come of your prayer. All you have done, actually, is given him another discouragment and, perhaps, closed the door to any future healing. If a person believes, he will ask for prayer, and if he doesn't ask, I usually wait until he does.

There are exceptions, of course. If you are led of the Spirit to inquire, do so and go from there expecting things to happen. The thing we have to remember, above all else, is the purpose of a God-given gift such as healing. We are empowered to be witnesses of the power of God for the purpose of saving souls. We are not running a portable hospital or competing with doctors. God also works through the doctors to bring about healing.

Jesus Christ is interested, too, in good family relationships. Several people have come to me at the prayer meetings and complained, "Pastor, I can't get my wife to come with me to these meetings, and I can't get her to go with me to worship services on Sundays." Or it is the wife complaining about the husband. I tell them very plainly, "This is no great problem. If you want to follow the simple plan of our Lord, you can change this." The secret, of course, is in following the divine directives, the divine plan. It works! The first rule comes in three parts: Don't nag. No spouse chased another spouse into the kingdom! The second one is: Don't nag! If you can't stop nagging, you might as well forget the rest of these rules. And the third part of the first rule is: *Don't nag!*

The second rule is: Love them! Even when

they are completely unlovable, love them. Anybody can love a lovely person when he or she *is* lovable, but it takes the grace of God to love another when he is being totally unlovely! When a man comes home from work after a bad day and blows his stack over some little thing, love him! At first he will be more than a little suspicious when the spouse doesn't respond in like manner. Eventually he will understand that she really does love him, even when he is not lovable, and he will be impressed.

It works equally well when the wife begins a tirade against her husband, and he loves her anyway, with a soft caress and a kiss. This is the new commandment, you will remember, that Christ gave to all Christians: "Love one another!" And note that it is not optional; it is a command. One of the greatest things about the charismatic renewal is that people really love one another. It is not part of a game; it is a beautiful reality.

The third rule is: Pray for them! And don't inaugurate the prayer program by pointing an accusing finger at them and announcing, "I am going to pray for you!" Under that kind of circumstance, it is little more than a threat and a demonstration of a sense of superiority. It is in the quiet time of prayer when you and God are alone that you should offer up your spouse into the sure hands of the One who promised, "With God all things are possible!"

How many times these complaining spouses have come back later, together, and said, "Pastor Wogen, I would like to have you meet my husband"; or, "my wife." And together they would attend regularly at Sunday worship services. They verify what Jesus said, "You have not, because you ask not. Ask and it shall be given."

At one time it was said that in the United States, Christianity had been tried and found "wanting." This is not true, for up to that time it had not been tried. It was "tried" in the Apostolic church, when they said of the early Christians, "Behold, how they love one another!" And at that time, when they *really* loved one another, they "turned the world upside down!" This is what Jesus Christ still is doing through the power of His Holy Spirit.

The Spirit walk is also a discovery of the Bible as God's word for today. Each day through the twenty-six years of my ministry prior to the baptism, I would in my own personal devotion faithfully try to read one chapter of the Bible, after which I would pray for the special needs of the members of the congregation and others. Then I would push the Bible aside and go to work feeling, "Now I am going to get things done!"

But there were days when I failed to perform my morning prayers, so I built myself an altar and bought myself a supply of twenty-four-hour votive candles. I would change the candle after I had prayed. It was a disciplinary thing: if the candle went out, it was because I had not prayed and read my scripture for the day. It was discouraging how many times the candle on the altar died of itself! After the baptism, they seldom died. I had a new love for the Scriptures, and I would not limit myself to one chapter but sometimes, if it was not too long, I would read the whole book! And it didn't rob me of the time to care for the needs of the congregation. I found myself living in the presence of God, and nothing can be more satisfying than that.

The Spirit walk is filled with delightful surprises—like the one that occurred the evening our calling team went to the home of a young couple. We knew only their names and address, but as soon as the introductions were over, all at once I said to the young man, "You are a wrestler." He gave me a strange look and said, "Yes, I am a wrestler."

There was no way I could have known that, and it bothered him, but it also created in him a desire to get some questions answered. He asked questions, and I answered them for two hours when I finally told him I was sorry but we had to go. This was our initial visit, and we never intended to spend more than twenty minutes on the first call. He answered, "Come back again. I want to talk to you some more!"

We came back in about ten days and were given a royal welcome. He said, "Say, we were talking about you last night." What made this man so interested? Because God had given me the word of knowledge that he was a wrestler. I heard no voice. I just simply *knew* without any reason for knowing. This is one of the gifts of the Spirit, one which gives us power to witness.

The Lord loves to deal with us in little things. On rainy days I have prayed for a parking spot right in front of the bank, and found one there. Many people have an experience like mine when I have misplaced something in the house, and then walked right to it, after I had prayed about it.

I used to have a Norwegian Elkhound named Rex that I kept in a kennel behind the parsonage. Two or three times a day I would let him out for exercise, and I would go about my business and come back later to put him in his pen. Sometimes I would forget or get involved in something else, and when I'd come to put him in, he would be gone. I would whistle and call and eventually he would return, but always he acted guilty; he would practically crawl around the end of the pen and scurry into the doghouse. Sometimes he would sneak in, and I wouldn't see him; then when I would look in the doghouse, he would be sitting there, worrying about what might happen to him.

One day I had let Rex out and waited too long. He really was gone. I called and whistled, but no dog. I had so many things to do that I had no time to wait for him; so I walked through the French doors off the patio, and putting my books on the table, I turned to God in prayer. "Lord," I said, "you know exactly how much work I have to do today, and you know I don't have time to stand around here and wait for my dog. Will you please send him back?"

I turned from my prayer and walked out in the backyard. There stood Rex, right in the middle of the yard. He was standing as though he were in a dog show, his tail curled over his back, ears alert, and his head up and tilted slightly to the side. Every inch of that dog said, "There is something funny going on around here!" There was indeed: God had never brought him back before!

And this is one of the beautiful things I have learned about our Lord: He loves to do little things as well as big things for us. I don't have to wait for a disaster before I turn to Him in prayer. For He is not only the Lord and Maker of the infinite, but of the infinitesimal. Each snow crystal has its own unique design; no two leaves are the same; no two trees are alike; no persons have been duplicated since the creation of the world. God even has an interest in how many hairs there are on your head.

He wants to be involved in little things, even to counting the sparrows one by one.

Created in His image, we are like that in lesser degree. We want, to be involved in giving small treats to our children. We do not want to wait around and be involved only in the great crises of our family. We have a tendency to regard God as we do the fire department: on call only in case of fire. We do our God a great injustice by denying Him the privilege of being our Father in the trivia of life as well.

The Spirit walk can lead us to a point where we know there is nothing too big and nothing too small for His hand to deal with. Like Paul, we, too, can say, "I know him in whom I have believed, and I am persuaded that he is able!"

The Spirit walk is a total life thing, to be desired by every Christian, for it is a source of inspiration and joy. Open your heart and seek it. It is God's plan for the final campaign for the kingdom!

CHAPTER 5

One of the most beautiful things awaiting those who embark on the Spirit walk is that denominational backgrounds, which once may have seemed so sharply defined and important, become in any group of charismatics virtually indistinguishable. There is no way to identify a person's church background without asking him, so completely transcendent is the renewing work of the Holy Spirit.

Which is not to say that there's anything wrong with denominational identity or worship. I am a Spirit-filled Christian who happens to be a Lutheran. I still prefer to worship in a Lutheran service, because that was the way I was brought up, but I have enjoyed and found peace in the strong presence of the Lord in every kind of service from a charismatic mass to a Pentecostal prayer and praise meeting. For we are *one* in the Spirit and *one* in the Lord.

Members from all of the divisions of the

Church have received the gifts of the Spirit. They speak in tongues; through them God heals the sick and speaks in prophecy; they are given words of wisdom, and have great faith. And through them God even performs miracles. They have and demonstrate the fruit of the Spirit— love, joy, peace, long-suffering, gentleness, goodness, faith, meekness, and temperance. Truly, there is not a choice between us.

What is God trying to do, destroy the different denominations? Not at all; He knows our fondness for our cherished traditions, many of which were divinely inspired in the first place. He is seeking by His Spirit to raise us up out of ourselves, to unite with Him and truly become the Body of Christ that we were intended to be. Jesus Christ is running the Church as He always has, and right now He is bringing denominations together—not to eliminate their churches, but to make them *one in the Spirit.*

An analogy might be made between the European Theatre in World War II and the move of the Spirit in the world today. When the Allies launched their campaign to conquer Europe, they did not invade the continent at once. They used dispersion tactics, putting small units in strategic locations over a wide area.

These soldiers were still intensely loyal to their own units and to their own kind. To a tanker, there is no soldier like a tanker; to an infantryman, no soldier like an infantryman;

to an artilleryman, no soldier like an artilleryman; and so on through the whole army. Each did his job in his area, loyal to his unit and proud to be a part of it.

But when the Allied Command came to the conclusion that it was time to roll across the continent and possess it, no one thought in terms of just his unit any more. All thought in terms of the Allied armies and the victory to be won. Overnight, these men became brothers in the conflict. They had a common commander and a common objective: peace for the world!

The Church of Jesus Christ has been engaged in "dispersion tactics" for four hundred and fifty years. Each church has been intensely loyal to its own unit. Each has served the cause of Christ well. Each has been faithful "to the heavenly vision." Now the "Allied Command," the Triune God—Father, Son and Holy Spirit—is bringing all the units together that all may benefit from the peculiar strengths of each and utilize them to the greater glory of Jesus Christ, the Commander of all of heaven's armies.

Though we know these are the last days and our world is not for long, we should suspend comparing one unit against another in the "Church Militant" until we are all gathered together in the "Church Triumphant." And it's doubtful our Commander will tolerate it then. I doubt very much that there will be a Lutheran Unit in heaven. But as long as there is a maximum spiritual effort called for here, it seems to be completely in line with sanctified common sense that we keep the Lutheran machinery functioning smoothly and in action.

What has our specific unit to offer? Lutheran tenacity and faithfulness in keeping Jesus Christ central in all of our programs and teachings, Lutheran insistence that all doctrine shall have its source in the Holy Scriptures, and the Gospel be kept in its original pure and simple form— these are vital to the Church Militant.

Sometimes, however, to the Lutheran Charismatic, what makes the Lutheran church great also makes her a little difficult to get along with—not impossible, just difficult.

For instance, there seems to be a reluctance to accept the word "baptism" in connection with the baptism with the Holy Spirit, and yet the Bible speaks repeatedly about the baptism with the Holy Spirit. There are other terms that can be used, such as "being filled with the Holy Spirit," but we cannot get away from the fact that Scripture does refer to this total immersion experience as a "baptism."

It is not so difficult to separate what the two "baptisms" do. Acts 1:8 states clearly, "You shall receive power, after that the Holy Spirit is come upon you, and you shall be witnesses unto me." The one is for the salvation of our souls and the other is for power to witness and to live the overcoming life that is the strongest witness of all. Though the same term is used, there is no duplication, no new order of salvation.

There is also a tendency on the part of some to insist that the baptism with the Holy Spirit and the various gifts of the Holy Spirit such as healing and miracles were only for the time of the Apostles. In Acts 2:17 we find Peter quoting the Old Testament prophet Joel, and fixing the timing of this experience as being "in the last days" and speaking of "prophesying" and "visions" and "dreams," all of which are occurring today among those who have received the baptism.

There need be no great concern about these things, because they are explained in Scripture and verified by the experiences of millions of persons in our day. I mention them only as an example of a difference of opinion. For the truth is, there is nothing in the experience that negates one single doctrine in the Lutheran church.

The thing to keep in mind here is that while there may be differences of opinion among those who haven't had the experience, there are no differences among those who have. And that is a significant number. On the basis of very conservative estimates today, there are over two thousand Lutheran pastors in the United

States who have received the baptism with the Holy Spirit, and there is no disagreement on these matters among them.

More important, I have not heard of a single one ever regretting the experience; on the contrary, their reactions run a positive gamut from quiet praise to outspoken exuberance. And these are trained Lutherans—cautious almost to a fault, hardly open to every wind of doctrine, but vulnerable to the truth.

There is no possible way of estimating the number of Lutheran lay people in the charismatic renewal, but there must be hundreds of thousands. I see them in every place I go all over the United States, Canada, Norway, Sweden, Denmark, Finland and Germany. After any meeting in whatever the country, they are quick to find their way down to the front and announce, "I am one of those Lutherans you were speaking about."

The number responding to the first and second International Lutheran Conference on the Holy Spirit, held in Minneapolis in August 1972 and 1973, is certainly an indication of Lutheran participation. There were more than ten thousand who attended at least one session at the first Conference, and over fifteen thousand at the second.

Of course, those present were not all Lutherans. As at all charismatic conferences, they came from practically every Christian body in the United States. I myself met many Lutherans at the two Catholic charismatic conferences I attended at Notre Dame. In fact, the discovery of their presence in such numbers was what first gave me the idea for an International Lutheran Conference.

One of the reasons the Lutherans are so open to the charismatic renewal is the hunger in their hearts for something more than they have. This spiritual hunger is universal. Our young people are leaving their churches by the thousands, and they are becoming involved in eastern religions, occult practices, and even witchcraft. Parents know the forces of evil that are running rampant in our land, and fear has sent them on a search. They expected to find the answer in the Lutheran church, and praise the Lord, that is where many are now finding it.

Some skeptics have tried to explain away the charismatic renewal as a psychiatric method. But psychiatry has not solved anything in or out of the charismatic field. It has only added another problem. All the Lutheran church has to do is to cling to its faith and its Bible and be open to the Spirit's leading. Luke 11:13 tells us, "If ye then, being evil, know how to give good gifts unto your children: how much more shall your heavenly Father give the Holy Spirit to them that ask Him!"

I predict that the charismatic renewal will

prove to be just that: the source and fountain
of badly needed renewal for all synods of the
Lutheran church and any other denomination
whose members include many believers hunger-
ing for a deeper walk with Christ.

CHAPTER 6

When Garland Eastham told me in Fort Lauderdale in January of 1970 that God would use me to bring charismatic renewal to the Lutherans, it was all I could do to keep from scoffing out loud. I have since learned that in Him all things really are possible and He really does use the foolish things of the world to confound the wise.

Late in 1970—in fact, between Christmas and New Year's—my wife and I had been visiting relatives in Minneapolis. We had planned to go home Wednesday afternoon, yet for some reason, I felt that we should stay a day longer. I mentioned it to my wife, and she was agreeable, so we stayed.

I then remembered that at this time the Lutheran Youth Encounter usually had a rally for young people at the Radisson Hotel downtown. I had the feeling that I should go there, and I did. There was good fellowship after the meeting, and for the first time I shared an idea that had been on my mind for some time: I mentioned to one of the adult leaders that there should be a Charismatic Conference for Lutherans.

Later, this man stopped me in the hall and introduced me to several others as they came from the meeting. Again I mentioned the idea for a Charismatic Conference for Lutherans, and they became excited at the prospect. Caught up in enthusiasm, we scheduled a meeting to discuss it on the following Tuesday at the Lutheran Youth Encounter offices.

The next morning Satan was again ready with his bucket: who did I think I was, even contemplating organizing a charismatic meeting for the whole Lutheran church? Why, there were eminent scholars among the ranks of charismatic Lutherans, and famous pastors and authors, men with far more experience and influence than a small-town farmboy pastor named Wogen. I must be out of my mind!

But, you know, one of the blessings of having the Spirit dwelling within is that you actually come to believe that all things *are* possible to God. Because He, not you, is the one who does it. All you have to do is listen, trust, and obey.

I began to share the vision with renewed enthusiasm. The idea appealed to others, and soon we had about sixteen men—pastors and lay people—attending. I was accepted as the president, and another meeting was set for the Curtis Hotel the following week. Never, before or since, have I conducted a meeting like that. The Holy Spirit was in charge from beginning to end.

Knowing that the business manager of Central Lutheran Church was a Charismatic, we first thought there would be a possibility of using the facilities of that church for a conference. It seemed particularly appropriate because it had an auditorium that seated twenty-five hundred people.

One of the men left the meeting to call them and he came back with the report, "We can't have Central." Instead of disappointment, with one voice everyone in the room said, "It's too small anyway." No one was wringing his hands in despair; the Lord didn't want us there.

Suddenly someone said, "Well, all right, why not the Minneapolis auditorium? There were several gasps; the auditorium seated 8,600! Well, why not? If God didn't want us to have it, all He had to do was close the door!

The same man left to telephone. He was gone for some time and then he rushed in, grinning from ear to ear. "We've got the auditorium!" Without a word, every voice broke out spontaneously singing the doxology: "Praise God from whom all blessings flow!"

There were a number of major points that we voted on that day: the date, the place, the financing, etc. And every decision was unanimous, followed by a song of praise. When we came to the question of financing, one of the men remarked, "Well, since it is the Holy Spirit's conference, and there's no way any of us could come up with that kind of money ourselves, why not let Him pay for it? Let's not have a registration fee—just free-will offerings."

That was one of the points covered by a unanimous vote. As the president, and not too sure that we should depend solely on the offering, I hesitated a little, then voted with the rest. We were going to have to spend a lot of money for the auditorium: publicity, travel, hotels for the speakers, and a lot of other things; but we discovered just how much the Lord is able! And only by letting us walk through it could He teach us to trust Him implicitly.

In a relatively short time seven main speakers were selected: Catholic, Father Edward O'Connor from the School of Theology at Notre Dame; a Lutheran pastor, Herbert Mjorud; and Episcopalian, Father Dennis Bennett from Seattle; a Pentecostal, Dr. David du Plessis, known as Mr. Pentecostal of the world, from South Africa; a Baptist pastor, Kenneth Pagard from Chula Vista, California; a European Lutheran pastor, Hans Jacob Frøen from Oslo, Norway; and a Presbyterian pastor, Mel Tari, from Indonesia. The reason for such diversity of speakers was precisely to let Christendom, and especially the Lutherans, know just how widespread and ecumenical the charismatic renewal was. We called it the International Lutheran Conference on the Holy Spirit, because we wanted to draw out the secret Lutheran Charismatics and bring them shoulder to shoulder with other Christians who knew something about the power of the Holy Spirit.

For example, I knew of one Lutheran pastor and his wife who had both received the baptism with the Holy Spirit but did not dare tell their congregation or anyone else for fear of being ejected from the parish and denied the privilege of another call. But I John 4:18 declares, "Perfect love casts out fear." And that was one thing there was sure to be an abundance of at the conference—love!

The names of the Spirit-filled pastors who agreed to handle the nineteen workshops were soon listed. Almost invariably as I called each man on the telephone and told him who I was and asked him to lead a certain workshop, his first three words were "Praise the Lord!" It was as if each man had been sitting on the edge of his chair waiting for this phone call. If I'd ever doubted whether the Lord had called the meeting, my last doubts were banished. Enthusiasm was universal and overwhelming. The night before the opening session, I was in a torment of doubt. The number of reservations was encouraging, but we were still heavily dependent upon the turnout of those within driving distance. Would there be enough to at least partly fill the auditorium? Or would we be faced with the spectre of bank upon bank of empty seats? Would we cover the costs of the conference? Would the program go smoothly?

In the end, all I could do was trust God—which was exactly what He wanted me to do, for He was in charge. And this He proceeded to demonstrate the next day.

We were dumbfounded most of that first day, the attendance was so large and the response so enthusiastic. The headlines on the front page of the Minneapolis *Star* said it all: GOD'S ELECTRICITY HITS THE CITY! And there were several pictures of the conference and healings.

But the thing that everyone noticed the minute he or she entered the halls of the conference was the incredible sensation of being enveloped in a cloud of love. We knew joy and unity and peace and kindness and mutual understanding far beyond the experience of anyone there. Truly the Lord was in that place with His power and blessings!

"Resist the devil, and he will flee from you," James says, We proved it one evening, early in the conference. All of a sudden a man stood up and began screaming and carrying on like a madman, flailing out at those around him.

He was located in the next to the top row of seats in the balcony on the right side, facing the stage, and he was plainly visible to the entire audience. Two of our men went to him, and in their authority as blood-bought children of the Lamb and in the name of Jesus they commanded the evil spirit to depart from him. It did, the man returned to his seat at peace and thanking God, and seven thousand people broke into thunderous applause! A shiver went down my spine. We had together witnessed a triumphant enactment of the spiritual warfare Martin Luther had so vividly depicted in his hymn, "A Mighty Fortress," more than four centuries earlier.

> And though His world, with devils filled,
>   Should threaten to undo us,
> We will not fear, for God hath willed
>   His truth to triumph through us:
>   The prince of darkness grim,
>   We tremble not for him;
>   His rage we can endure,
>   For lo! his doom is sure,
>   One little word shall fell him.
> That Word above all earthly powers,
>   No thanks to them abideth;
> The Spirit and the gifts are ours
>   Through Him who with us sideth . . .

The word, of course, was Jesus, and that night it did abide above all our earthly goings-on. And that night the Spirit and the gifts were received by dozens. A lady from Winona, Minnesota, later told me that she and four other women from that town drove to Minneapolis to find out what the Lutheran Conference on the Holy Spirit was all about. She said every last one of them received the baptism with the Holy Spirit before they went home.

She also told about being in one of the halls and seeing a young man going by on crutches. He wasn't doing too well, but he found his way into the room where people were being prayed for, for healing. His wife went with him to help him. The five ladies were still in the hallway when the man came out. His wife was carrying one of his crutches, and he was walking as well as any man and swinging the other on his finger and singing, "Praise God! Praise God!"

As Paul commanded the believers of Ephesus (Eph. 5:18), hundreds of people received the baptism with the Holy Spirit in the auditorium during the week, and there were reports each day of sixty, forty, and fifty people receiving the baptism in the Curtis Hotel following the meetings. I have no idea how many times Acts 19:1-6 was reenacted (where Paul, when he finds that the Ephesians have not received the Holy Spirit, lays hands on them and they do), but there had been prayer that three thousand people might receive the baptism during the conference, and that figure may be entirely accurate.

After one of the last programs, a lady who

had been in the audience reported that she had seen a vision. "When the man began the opening devotions this evening, I saw a brilliant light above the stage, and under the light was a fierce eagle. Under the eagle were three fish arranged in a row. Under the row of fish were three doves. And under the three doves there were three golden circles. As the man continued to pray, the three fish came together, and there was one fish. The three doves came together, and there was one dove. And the three golden circles became interlocked, like the symbol of the Trinity!" After she related it, I gave her what I thought was the interpretation, "The three fish represent the three Lutheran bodies at the Conference, ALC, LCA, and LC Missouri Synod, and they have truly become 'one in the Lord.' The three doves coming together represent the fact that they are now one in the spirit. The three circles indicate the fact that we are all three Lutheran bodies, but we are locked together in the Spirit. The fierce eagle over it all represents the majesty and power of the Lord who is Master of it all."

The overall picture of the first International Lutheran Conference could be given in the words of Christ, "The blind saw, the lame walked, the deaf heard, and the poor had the Gospel preached to them." And the Lutherans and many other Christians all over the world became aware of a new dimension in Christianity—the dimension of the Spirit.

CHAPTER 7

One day in the summer of '72 I felt moved to go to Green Lake, Wisconsin, for a Full Gospel Business Men's Fellowship retreat, though I did not know of anyone who was going to be there, or any of the speakers. The only thing I did know about these retreats was that they were usually very fulfilling.

I arrived in Green Lake after a 250-mile drive in my VW, on a Thursday evening, attended a small prayer meeting that evening and went to bed very tired. Friday morning, Henry Carlson, the man in charge, asked me if I would give a five-minute greeting. I did, and it seemed to go all right. After the greeting he asked if I would give a talk that afternoon. Surprised, yet again sensing the shadow of God's hand, I asked, "What kind of a talk do you want? How long do you want me to speak?"

"Oh, you know, an hour or an hour and a half."

Well, you know Lutheran preachers don't talk that long. But by his answer, I felt I knew what he and the Lord wanted.

That afternoon I shared with some two hundred men the experiences that had led me to Fort Lauderdale and what had happened afterwards. Then Chairman Carlson announced, "I think Pastor Wogen will be going with us on our spring airlift to Scandinavia."

Scandinavia? Airlift? What in the world was he talking about?

I was still puzzling over that one when a little later he made another announcement, "Well, it's definite: Pastor Wogen will be going with us on our airlift to Scandinavia! One of the men just gave me a check for his passage."

No one had spoken to me in the interim, no one told me what an "airlift" was, and no one had asked me if I was available. But this is the way the Spirit often moves. Chairman Carlson had gotten a leading that possibly I was one of the men who was to go with them to the Scandinavian countries. He laid the possibility before the group, and the confirmation came in the form of a check.

Thus was he sure it was the Holy Spirit's plan that I go, and for him to have asked me, "Are you available and will you go?" would have been a waste of breath. The Holy Spirit had planned it—even bringing me from Cedar Rapids to Green Lake Bible Camp. The only thing left was for me to learn when and from which airport we would be leaving. As it turned out, we were to leave from New York the coming April and fly direct to Copenhagen, Denmark. I wished Merna could go, but she was unable to leave her teaching job and said she would be just as happy to stay home and support me in prayer.

For some strange reason, I found myself a rather lonely fellow as we got on the plane in New York. I would have been almost as pleased to get another plane, going home. What was I doing here? Could this really be of the Lord? Or was I kidding myself?

But I was committed on some other man's money. And so I sat in the huge plane and watched other passengers board, and got progressively lonelier—until a pleasant fellow named Chester sat down next to me.

I learned that an airlift was a group of Spirit-filled men going abroad to hold meetings, to witness, to fellowship, and in general to be available to the Holy Spirit for whatever use He would put them to. Before we landed in Copenhagen, we had discussed many aspects of the charismatic renewal and were becoming honest with one another. This conversation got into divine healing, and just about everything. "But this leg-lengthening business, that I don't buy!" "I'm with you," I replied. "I don't buy it either. It seems that when they don't have anything else to pray for, then it's 'Let's lengthen a few legs' ! ''

This I have discovered: you can be perfectly honest with the Lord. If you don't believe something, you can say so. The sky won't fall! But what may happen is that the Lord will make a believer of you. That very evening, at a service for some 600 people in an auditorium in Copenhagen, I found myself one of three men on the stage besides the speaker, Pastor Joe Poppel. When he asked for people to come up to be prayed for, a lady came up using two sturdy canes and with practically everything visibly wrong with her. Joe Poppel had her sit on a chair, and he lifted her feet up so that he could check the length of her legs. One of the legs was nearly two inches shorter than the other. Joe asked, "Shall we believe the Lord for the lengthening of this leg?" Then he began to pray.

I had already made up my mind that this I was going to see and find out if it was real. The prayer had scarcely begun when the shorter leg came out as though it had been telescoped! There was no movement of the woman's hips, no manipulation of anything that could give the impression of the leg growing out. It literally grew out right in front of my eyes!

It was as though the Lord was asking me, "All right, Wogen, did you see that?" And I had to admit that I had. It was real.

To make the lesson still more indelible, the next lady to come to the stage had a wizened left shoulder, and her left arm was at least an inch shorter than the other. Again Joe asked, "Shall we believe the Lord for the lengthening of this arm?"

He had not prayed long before that arm literally shot out the length that it was short, and the lady cried out when it happened. Again, it was as though the Lord was saying, "Wogen, did you see that?" And while this time it had happened so quickly I couldn't see it, no one could deny the validity or completeness of the healing.

So if you have a doubt, go ahead and express it. It amounts to an invitation for Him to teach you. But don't parade your disbelief before everyone, as if to prove there is no God. That would be defiance and not doubt.

We Lutherans—and if the shoe fits, put it on, even if you're not a Lutheran—put so much stock in faith and are so fearful we don't have enough that I get the impression people think we have to "cook up our own bag of faith." Not so! Faith is a gift! If you're short on faith, ask for more, and you'll get it! As Paul wrote to the Christians at Ephesus, "For by grace are ye saved through faith; and that not of yourselves: it is the gift of God."

Do you remember what Jesus said to the man who wanted his son to be delivered from the demon? He said, "All things are possible to them that believe." And then do you remember what the Lord did? He gave the man faith to believe, and his son was delivered.

There were one hundred fifty-five men on the airlift to Scandinavia. The second night we were in Copenhagen a Catholic priest, Father George De Prizio, and I preached in a Lutheran church, where the pastor and many of the members were charismatic. The church was packed! We used interpreters, of course, as we didn't know the Danish language, but we needed no interpreter to discern the spirit in that crowd! It makes no difference as to country or language: there is a spirit of love and warmth in a charismatic congregation that is just not found in any other.

From Copenhagen we fanned out to all parts of Europe. My team went to southern Sweden, to a small charismatic Bible school where we spent a few days, and then to another Christian school of about 200 students. Everywhere we went there was a real hunger for spiritual things. One young pastor wanted us to come back and establish a training center at the school so that its pastors could experience this special blessing and Spirit, but the language barrier made it impractical.

The school where we spent most of our time in southern Sweden was run by a charismatic couple. They owned three houses, in which they fed, housed, and taught the students—and paid the entire bill. The man owned a small manufacturing plant in that village, in which he did most of the work, too. That kind of devotion and sacrifice reflects credit on the charismatic renewal, no matter what the country.

The airlift regathered in Stockholm for a few days prior to going back to the States. There was a big banquet in the Grand Hotel, attended by around five hundred people. There were people present from all over Europe, and their warmth and enthusiasm was something that will be long remembered.

I spoke at one of the Lutheran churches in Stockholm, and when I asked those who wanted to be prayed for to come forward, among them was a tall man in a dark grey business suit. He was impeccably dressed, good looking, the perfect example of the successful executive. He threaded his way through the crowd, oblivious to everyone he passed in the aisle, and I discovered he spoke perfect English. I asked him, "What would you like from the Lord tonight?"

"I would like to know what this Gospel is that they are talking about."

I spoke to him about his need of a Savior. I prayed that he would see how needy he really was, for on the surface he seemed eminently respectable with much that the world had to offer. But he repeated the sinner's prayer after

me, solemnly and thoughtfully accepting Christ
as his Savior and Lord. I congratulated him and
said, "Now you are a member of God's kingdom!
Would you like the baptism with the Holy Spirit?"

"Yes," he said, after a moment, "I think
I would like that, too." And he received.

When he came up to the altar, he was a sad
and lonely man. He had lost his wife about six
months before. When he went out, he was a
completely new man. He wore a radiant smile
and greeted everyone he passed. The influence
of this witness only God knows, but I have a
feeling that the Lord is putting him to good use
in Stockholm.

I remember an invitation I received to come
to one of the most fashionable Lutheran churches in Stockholm. Its pastor is an ordained woman, Pastor Margit Sahlin, and she has two ordained women working with her. I don't know
why, but I somehow expected to meet a short,
fat, jolly woman, and was startled instead to
meet one of the most intelligent and beautifully
poised women in Sweden. The interpreter was
asked to come early, too. He turned out to be
equally impressive, as well as one of the most
respected members of the Swedish parliament.
When Sweden has a subject to put before the
United Nations in New York, this is the man
who makes the presentation.

Pastor Sahlin had made a special effort to

invite a number of the leaders from the various congregations nearby to hear me, thus assuring a most receptive audience. Indeed, there was a sustained interest throughout the evening.

But perhaps the most moving event that happened to me personally occurred the night that one of the men who served as my interpreter invited me to his home for a late supper following an evening meeting. It was a beautiful, tastefully furnished home, and the food and fellowship were delicious and delightful. At the end of the evening, the man asked his wife to bring him his checkbook, and he proceeded to write a check to me for five hundred kroner (about $125 in American dollars). In addition, he also paid for one week's lodging at the hotel and my meals.

It was hard to say who was the more grateful, for mine has been a faith mission. I have received no salary for the past year and a half. I resigned from my parish October 1, 1972. There was no trouble in the congregation, and it was not necessary that I leave. It was a matter of God's leading me to take that step, as I was getting involved with conferences and speaking engagements across the country.

The day before we left Sweden for home, Dr. Leland Paulson, a Bible teacher from Chicago, and I were assigned to hold a seminar in Gustav Vasa Church in Stockholm. I have seen St. Peter's and the Sistine Chapel in Rome, and many beautiful churches across the European continent and the United States, but in my opinion none compares with the beauty of Gustav Vasa Church in Stockholm. Dr. Paulson, a Pentecostal, was to present the basics of the charismatic renewal, and I was to present the same topic from the Lutheran point of view. We were told there would be between forty and fifty people present, as it was going to be on Monday afternoon. A question and answer period was to follow.

There were nearly two hundred people present, and when it was time for questions from the floor, there were none. Dr. Paulson, sitting in the front pew, suggested I give an altar call.

I had never given an altar call up to that point, so I said, "You give the altar call." But again he urged that I do it. So I simply told the audience, "Almighty God is present here in this church with all of His power. If any of you here are suffering in any area of your being —body, soul or spirit—we would like to have you come to the altar, and we will pray for you."

About seventy-five people came forward—in fact, there were so many that they extended into the chancel area, and we had to call upon every Spirit-filled man or woman present to come and assist.

I have never felt the power of God more strongly than I did in Gustav Vasa that Monday afternoon. Periodically it was as though I were being charged with an electric wire in the middle of my back; the power would flow through me to the ones I was praying for. At one point as I put my hand on the head of a lady who was suffering from cancer, she cried out as the power went through her. She was completely healed of her cancer. All kinds of healings took place in the chancel area. Many were "slain in the Spirit" and would drop to the floor. And many received the baptism with the Holy Spirit.

Reports reached us afterward, from people living in Stockholm, that there were probably more miracles taking place in the pews than we witnessed at the altar. Cripples with crooked legs were healed instantly. People with braces on their legs took them off, having no further need for them. Some with large goiters on their necks felt them disappear. Crooked and aching backs were straightened, and pain left them.

In working for the Lord, there is no way to anticipate what is going to happen. Sometimes when everything seems to be just right, nothing extraordinary happens, at least on the outside. At other times, in the middle of what seems to be just presentation with no great miracles, suddenly the Spirit takes over and everything happens. Why? I don't know. Perhaps because the whole thing is 100 percent up to God and 0 percent up to us, and He would have us keep that ever in mind. All we can do—all we are supposed to do—is be obedient.

Towards the end of our stay, I asked a Swedish Lutheran pastor about a report that there were one thousand charismatic prayer groups in Stockholm. I found it hard to believe.

"Oh well, I would say there are at least that many," he answered, without thinking anything of it.

In one city there are one thousand charismatic prayer groups! Sweden's very worldly way of life is well known, but she is like a desert, thirsting for water. When water is poured on the desert, it blooms almost instantly, and when the Spirit falls on a spiritually dry country, overnight a spiritual garden blooms. Scandinavia is on fire! She has been lighted by the Spirit of the living God, and she is witnessing to the world.

It takes about nine hours by plane from Stockholm back to the States, and there were no "sleepers" on the way back. Everyone was sharing, and no one was left without a treasure of experiences to tell. The plane load of men and women was as enthusiastic as the seventy whom Jesus sent out, "Lord, even the devils were subject unto us in your name!"

America, too, needs to hear the voice of God this day, as He speaks to the nations in II Chronicles 7:14, "If my people, which are called by my name, shall humble themselves, and pray, and seek my face, and turn from their wicked ways; then will I hear from heaven, and will forgive their sin, and will heal their land."

Sweden is a good example of what God will do when a people lift their voices to Him in prayer. May the Holy Spirit continue to burn right across the country until every soul is alive to this marvelous light of life!

CHAPTER 8

While I was in Scandinavia, I was invited by a group of charismatic Lutherans in Finland to return to Helsinki two months later for Pentecost, after which I would go to Stockholm and then to Darmstadt, and other cities around Germany. I became acquainted with a young man who was stationed with the Campus Crusade in Frankfurt. He gave me his phone number and said I should call him when I came to town, and that he would provide me with bed and board for a few days.

Later, when I did get to Frankfurt and made the call, he was most apologetic, saying, "I have wall-to-wall Indians, and I can't do a thing for you. A whole group of them came in last night from India, and we are jammed to capacity. But I will give you two telephone numbers; call them in this order."

I called the first number and asked for a place to stay, telling the woman who answered that I was a charismatic Lutheran from the States. She asked me to call back in ten minutes. When I called back, she assured me I would be most welcome, and gave me directions to the place. It involved a bus ride and then a taxi.

I had no idea where I was going, only an address. When I stepped out of the taxi I saw in huge letters, "Canaan." Canaan in Darmstadt? Then it dawned on me where I was. I was at the Lutheran Convent of the Sisters of Mary, the home of Mother Basilea Schlink and Mother Martyria and about one hundred and twenty-five other sisters. They were most kind and gracious, and every one of them had been baptized with the Holy Spirit.

This was one of those unique incidents that the Lord tucks into His people's lives from time to time. Almost everything about their life had a little ceremony to it. We were awakened by the sisters' singing. Quiet hours were observed as a part of each day.

Canaan in Darmstadt is a monument of miracles built by the faith and the hands of these dedicated sisters. They had been told there was no way they could expect to obtain that property because the government was going to put a freeway through there. But the sisters persisted, and God miraculously arranged for them to get their chosen site. With their own hands they began to prepare the ground. Mother Basilea had been given a vision as to what the finished plan would look like. It included a small lake with a gushing fountain nearby and lovely trees and flowers. The sisters proceeded with the plans according to the vision of Mother Basilea.

But when she contacted a welldriller to put in the well, she was informed that there was a dry pocket where the property stood; there would be no water available. Mother Basilea insisted, until finally, to prove to her there was no water there, the man drilled the well. To his complete astonishment, he struck water, and the well produced twenty-five times as much water as any he had ever drilled. God's faithfulness was in my ears the entire time I spent in Canaan, because about seventy-five yards from the window of my room, night and day, I could hear the soothing sound of the fountain.

For little or nothing the sisters received several truck loads of cobblestones from the old road the highway construction company was replacing. These stone cubes the sisters patiently laid one by one on what would be the lake bottom. It was located exactly so that when the well came in, the lake was soon filled. The women prepared a garden with a walkway through it, and scenes from the life of Christ in life-size statuary were placed along the path. There were beautiful quiet places, too, where a visitor could sit and meditate.

Visitors from eleven different countries were there. They came from as far away as Australia, Iceland, and of course, the United States. Classes were held each day at certain hours, and earphones with simultaneous translation were provided for those who couldn't understand German, by interpreters, located in their own soundproof rooms. Everything went so smoothly and gracefully that few guests could have realized how much work had gone into the accomplishment of each day's program.

As long as I was there, I asked Sister Pesta if I might have an interview with Mother Basilea. She was surprised at my request, "But Mother Basilea is sick in bed." I knew that, but pointed out that as a pastor, I had called on any numbers of ladies who were sick in bed. While I had hoped some arrangement might be possible, I didn't press the point.

Later, Sister Pesta (who was the equivalent of the sergeant major of the Sisterhood) informed me, "Mother Martyria will see you this afternoon at three." And promptly at three, I was ushered into a small room with two chairs. Soon Mother Martyria, who with Mother Basilea presided over the Convent, appeared. She had a rather stern appearance at all times, and her hair was drawn severely back and tied in a small knot in the back. She was all business.

"Pastor Wogen, I did not agree to see you because you are Pastor Wogen. I wanted to see you because I am thinking of the several thousand people you are going to be leading at the next Lutheran Conference in Minneapolis." We discussed various things about the conference and Canaan, but I sensed there was something on her mind, and she was preparing me for it.

Finally she said, "Pastor Wogen, there is something I have to say, and I want you to know I tell you this in love. I must tell you that you are a very vain man."

I don't know how many people you have had look you in the eye and tell you that you are a "very vain person." It was my first time. I did not resent it, for she did it as a duty. I have since thought about this a great many times. What makes a man appear vain to another person? If I appeared so, I didn't want to—nor did I want to be *vain*. Those at Canaan are, of course, totally devoid of vanity, so I assume even a little was very bad. I will always be thankful to Mother Martyria for this bit of criticism, and I believe it helped me.

There were many beautiful things that happened while I was there, and I have not even begun to describe the beauty and serenity of the place. But after four days, I left to journey north to Braunschweig.

The first meeting in Braunschweig that I

was asked to lead was held in the Catholic Church of the Holy Spirit, a lovely little church. The priest was one of the sweetest men I have ever met. He hugged me with great feeling, then kissed me on both cheeks. Then he kissed me on the back of the hands and looked me in the eyes and said, "Pastor Wogen, I love you."

The church was filled to capacity with charismatic people, and we had a beautiful meeting. When you speak to a charismatic group, you have a room full of shining eyes looking at you, and a little smile on each face. And you have their undivided attention, too.

As I spoke I was conscious of a man, with a dark look about him, hovering on the fringe of things. He didn't bother me, but I was conscious of him. When the altar call was given and dozens of people came up to be prayed for, I noticed he was still standing at the back. Later, another man was talking to him, and when I looked up, he motioned that I should come over to him.

When I reached him I asked him, "Did you want to be prayed for?"

"Oh, no," he answered, "I have a message for you: You are to launch out into the other gifts of the Spirit and not just use the ones you were using tonight."

I recognized the spirit from which the message came, and it wasn't the Holy Spirit! I thanked him and went back to praying for people.

After the meeting I asked the regular members of the prayer group if any of them knew this man. But none of them had ever seen him before. They also told me many things about Braunschweig: that this was where Hitler had gotten his start. This was the town where he pulled down the first cross from the steeple of a church and ran up the Swastika. This was where he used to come back and consult with demon-possessed women as to how to run Germany. Some even suggested there might be witches flying around the Hartz mountains south of the city. And it began to seem as though this could very well be the demon capital of that part of Europe.

There are effective ways of taking care of demons who may try to bother a meeting. The next night, the meeting was held in a school auditorium, and at the close of my opening prayer, I bound the spirits. I asked God to make them blind and deaf and dumb and throw them out of the hall. I had no more than concluded my prayer, when nine men got up and walked out. There were four younger men on either side with an older man in the middle. I wondered what I had said in my prayer. Had I offended them? You don't like to lose your audience before you begin to speak! Then it dawned on me that I had bound the spirits and kicked them out. And they were leaving.

Again, following the meeting, I asked those who seemed to be the elders of the group if any of them knew the nine who had walked out. None of them had seen any of them before. As envoys of the devil, they were there for no good. The one the previous night accomplished nothing. All Charismatics know that God says, in Romans 12:6, "Having, then, gifts differing according to the grace that is given us." God determines our gifts; we don't just take them. So the former envoy who had not accomplished his mission the first night sent nine men the second night.

The point is this: you don't have to put up with demons! Nor do you need to make a big thing of them. Some have told me that I oversimplify dealing with demons. I am told demons have names and rank, and they are in charge of certain sections of our country. Who said so? The demons said so. Do you know who the father of demons is? He is the father of all lies, and it would be rather foolish to believe one single word a demon tells you. Besides that, their rank means nothing because a private in the King's army can cast out any four-star general in the devil's army!

Bensheim, Germany, is another spot where a great work is being done by Charismatics. Much of it centers around the Teen Challenge Center, where I lived for four days. This was where I saw a three-year-old child who had received the baptism with the Spirit. That little girl was amazing in so many ways, but what was most noteworthy is that even at three years of age, a child can receive this gift.

Several rallies were held while I was there, with many experiencing healings or deliverance from drug habits, and several receiving the baptism with the Holy Spirit. Half the drug addicts that come to the Teen Challenge Center are American soldiers and half are German young people. Real Spirit-inspired love for one another has helped a great deal to turn hundreds to Christ and to eventual deliverance from drug addiction.

Again, this is a faith mission with very little support from the States, and a great deal of sacrifice on the part of the magnificent minority. One man, who had been with IBM for several years, and his wife had dedicated one year of their time and money to work with the people there. When the man had asked the IBM for a year's leave of absence, he was refused it. So he said, "Well, I suppose I will have to resign my job then, because we definitely feel we are supposed to do this." When he put it like that the company decided it could make an exception in his case, and he was given the year's leave of absence.

One night following a meeting in Bensheim, I was praying for several people who had stayed on. I put my hand on the head of a girl who had asked to be prayed for. As soon as I said, "In the name of Jesus," she literally went wild, striking out with her arms and nearly wrecking the amplifying system. I pulled her away from the amplifier to an uncluttered area where I could pray for her, and she was delivered of the demon in a short time.

I tell this incident—and there were many similar—because this was an intelligent and promising girl. In this area we are not dealing with "down-and outers," but with those who are "up-and comers."

When they are delivered, they become not only great witnesses of the power of Christ, but also counselors who can warn others of the hell of demon possession, which is a very real thing in our day.

One sees American young people traveling all over Europe. They need to know something more than a story of a loving God. They need to know Jesus Christ as their own personal Savior and Lord, who has the right and the wisdom to tell them what to do and what not to do. With the adventurous spirit of youth, it is easy to think they can try this or that, but if they dabble in drugs, sorcery, or any of the many mind-expanding, higher consciousness meditations, like "transcendentalism," occult practices, seance parties, Satan congregations, and the like, they are dealing with the world of evil forces—the enemies of Christ—and they may never know freedom again.

The devil does not come in a red suit, wearing horns and tail. He comes in many guises, even claiming the name of guru, an exalted one or holy man. Unless any group claiming supernatural power comes under the name of Jesus Christ, its members are courting death! Never in the history of the world has the devil conducted such an all-out compaign for the souls of men as he has today.

There is no better advise for our times than what the Apostle Paul gives in Ephesians 6:11-13, "Put on all of God's armor so that you will be able to stand safe against all strategies and tricks of Satan. For we are not fighting against people made of flesh and blood, but against persons without bodies—the evil rulers of the unseen world, those mighty satanic beings and great evil princes of darkness who rule this world; and against huge numbers of wicked spirits in the spirit world. So use every piece of God's armor to resist the enemy whenever he attacks, and when it is all over, you will still be standing up!"

CHAPTER 9

One day in December 1973, I received a telephone call from a man in Surrey, British Columbia, wanting to know if I could give his group some of my time. I told him I was not committed in January. "How much time do you want?"

"Well," he said, "I think we can use you for the month." I had never met this man. He knew very little about me, and yet he called and scheduled me for a month. This is what happens when one is walking in the Spirit.

Originally it was thought that I would go to Vancouver first, but one day I received a letter. "You are to go to Calgary first and then come out west."

He said a letter would follow, but I had to go to Denver for a couple of days, and then planned to go to Calgary and so did not receive a letter of instructions for Calgary. When I got there, I did not have the name of a pastor or a church. While waiting for someone to come and claim me, I met a young Catholic woman who was involved with retreats across the country, and we enjoyed sharing thoughts on the move of God's Spirit in our world.

When she left on another plane, I thought it was time that I did something about my own situation. Over the loudspeaker system I asked that someone come to a certain ticket counter. Within five minutes I heard a voice behind me, "Well, Norris, how are you?" Here was a friend, Harald Bredesen, whom I had not seen for over thirty years. He, too, was a charismatic speaker, traveling around the world.

We had a great time sharing, and it just happened that he also knew the name of the pastor and the name of the church where I would be working. I mention this just to indicate how completely delightful it is to work for the Lord. Although our paths had crossed in Stockholm, we had not met in all these years until I came to Canada. Later I had the opportunity of speaking in his church in Victoria.

I speak to any charismatic group anywhere, regardless of denomination, and I have learned to be at home with all of them. My main burden, however, continues to be for the Lutherans, naturally, as there are so many hundreds of thousands of them who are not yet involved in the charismatic renewal.

A definite pattern has developed: I speak to one of those other groups, and invariably there are some Lutherans who attend to find out what is going on. There we have a chance to meet and speak with one another, and then arrangements are made, by the Lutherans, for me to come back to the same area later under Lutheran sponsorship. Because of my black suit and clerical collar and, perhaps, my white hair, they identify with me. That, and the fact that I am somewhat reserved by nature, encourage these people as they begin to realize that they don't have to be excessively emotional nor aggressive in promoting the charismatic speakers. The Holy Spirit is a gentleman in the finest sense of the word, and He can accommodate himself to anyone.

The Lord has commanded us to "be all things to all men if, perchance, you might save some." The Holy Spirit does the same. If a person does not fit in one type of prayer group, that doesn't cancel out the Charismatic. You must find another, or start one from your own church and begin exercising the gifts the Spirit gives you.

The Canadians, I find, are of the same temperament that we are, and we have wonderful times together. They have a sincerity about them and a zeal that must be completely satisfying to the Lord. He is blessing them in so many ways, for the charismatic renewal is spreading rapidly across Canada. One Lutheran pastor I talked to, who was very concerned about anything in his congregation that might have a tendency to divide his people, came home one day and told his wife, "I am in favor of this charismatic renewal now."

"That's good," she told him, "because I've been speaking in tongues for two months now, and our oldest daughter received the baptism about six months ago!"

I spent a few days at a charismatic Bible camp near Caroline, Alberta, where the temperature reached forty-one degrees below zero while I was there. One morning before I was to speak, I became conscious of an acute stomach pain and wondered if I would be able to deliver the talk. Suddenly a Cree Indian made the announcement that there was a person in the room with a pain in his stomach.

"Step out and we will pray for you," he said calmly. I hesitated, thinking there might be someone else. He made the second invitation, and I still hesitated.

Then another man spoke up and said, "The person who has this pain should step out, as a confirmation of the faith of the one who was given the discernment." I stepped out then, into the center of the circle, and they prayed for me, and, of course, the pain left me immediately.

I spoke to the Indian later and he said, "I knew it was you, and if you hadn't stepped out, I would have spoken to you after the meeting."

Now that I have confessed my own slowness to respond, let me encourage *you* not to be slow in coming out. God wants to heal. But the step of faith in coming out seems to be very important. At many of Kathryn Kuhlman's meetings, people are in the process of being healed as they come toward the stage, but there are many more who hesitate; they have to be urged to come out. I am convinced that it is better to be the effervescent, spontaneous Peter than some kind of shrinking violet who isn't looking for anything great from the Lord. Expect great things from Him, for He is truly great!

I have made two trips to Canada already this year, and at least one more trip is scheduled. The one thing I am confident of is that the Lord is in charge. As long as this is true, we can expect great things to happen. But the most important thing is to let the Lord lead us and be sure that it is He who is doing the leading and not we ourselves. We can push on with a lot of things and never be fully certain we are moving in the right direction, but as surely as we are led of the Lord, we can relax and live on the edge of expectancy.

CHAPTER 10

Once recently in Illinois I was to preach at both morning services in a Missouri Synod Church. I asked the pastor what he wanted me to do. "I can go right down the bore, or I can beat around the bush," I said.

"You go right down the bore," he told me; "Preach Pentecost!"

"You may have some pieces to put together when I leave."

"I'll be here on Monday morning, and if there are any pieces to put together, I'll do it!" He said.

Fortunately, I had asked him to have a man stand behind each individual specifically asking for prayer after the service. Five or six of the members were "slain in the Spirit." One received a definite healing of her back, and several others received the baptism. I have received no reports of any difficulty in that church since then, and I am confident there is none.

Another time, after a meeting where I spoke in Milwaukee, one of my very good friends from the seminary and his wife came forward. "We just thought we would come tonight and let you know we are on your side," he told me. "We have received the baptism, too!"

You can't imagine the thrill of having another seminarian admit to this beautiful experience. I repeated to him what someone once told me, "You are the last one I expected to have this experience!" Which simply bears out again that we are not running this world. God is!

It was also in Wisconsin, but in a different town, that a young woman came to me before the program and asked if I would pray for her mother before my talk.

"That's putting the cart before the horse, isn't it? There's a definite order that we follow, as found in Mark 16:20: 'And they went forth, and preached everywhere, the Lord working with them and confirming the word with signs following.' " The Lord demonstrates in the healing of the body what He has already done in the soul. "Why can't the prayer for your mother follow the meeting?" I asked her.

"The longer she sits, the more terrible the pain becomes, and she can't stand it," the woman explained. "She has to leave!"

"All right," I said, "have her come forward; we will pray for her back."

The mother came forward, and we prayed that God would let her sit comfortably through the meeting, which He did. She had no pain at all. This was a nice prelude to the healing itself. She had a minor hunchback condition. I put my hands on her back and began to pray, and her back straightened. The pain was gone. Then she wanted the baptism, so I prayed with my hand on her head, and in just a few moments she was filled with the Spirit. What a beautiful evening of experiences for this lady, and how wonderful is our God who cares and heals every part of our being—body, soul and spirit!

I like to recall, too, a wonderful weekend in Aberdeen, South Dakota. The big meeting was in a large auditorium at a motor inn. The room was well filled, and the program was above average, with a good musical group and some testimonies. Following the meeting, several people came forward for prayers. There was an elderly lady who came using a tubular crutch. I asked her, "Do you think the Lord can heal you?"

"Yes, I believe the Lord can heal me," she said.

"That's fine," I said. "Do you believe the Lord *will* heal you right now?"

She answered, "Well, I know He can."

"That is not what I asked you," I reminded her. "Do you believe He will heal you right now?"

Then she answered, "Yes, I believe He will heal me right now."

"That's fine," I said. "Now let's pray."

After I had prayed a very short and simple prayer for healing, I asked her, "Will you stand up?" She started reaching for her crutch, and I said, "No, just stand up." She did. Then I said, "Take a little walk." She did that, too. Ask and believe; the Lord does the rest!

The lady next in line had her chin down on her chest. I asked what her problem was and she said, "I can't raise my chin." After asking her the same two questions I had asked the lady before her, she answered in the affirmative. We prayed a brief prayer.

Then I said, "Now lift up your head." And she did. Then I said, "Now raise it way up and swing your head from side to side." She did it with no difficulty.

A lady and her husband were next, both with the same kind of back problem. I am confident the lady's back was healed, but I am not sure the husband's was. Then she wanted the baptism, and in a few moments she received it! It is thrilling to watch the Lord work His wonders! Faith is the most important ingredient in the matter of healing, and apparently the Lord had been strengthening theirs throughout the meeting.

There is little opposition to the charismatic renewal in the Lutheran church today. Too many things have happened all over the United States and the rest of the world for anyone to doubt its validity. People are coming alive to the reality of changed lives, a body of people filled with love and peace and joy which has not been seen before in the history of the Lutheran church. Charismatic congregations are coming into their own; and where they are, there are no problems of finances, evangelism, or divisions within the congregation. One charismatic pastor declared that for the first time in his twenty years in the ministry, he had all his bills paid!

But the need of the hour is not so much for evangelists for the Holy Spirit, as for teachers who will keep the emphasis where God intended—on the person of Jesus Christ and the need of a deep, personal relationship with Him as the Savior and Lord.

American Charismatics have a great responsibility today. They dare not waver or break down in the face of whatever opposition they may meet. They must continue to study Scripture until, along with Paul, they come to the same conclusion he came to when he said, "I know him in whom I have believed, and I am persuaded that he is able to keep that which I have committed unto him against that day."

Surely no one can deny the fact that we are in the end times. The devil, the world, and our own flesh (to name our basic enemies) know we are in the end times. The feverish activity on the part of the devil and mankind in general that marks our day indicates we are in the end times. The increasing incidences of violence in nature and the promise of continued increase marks this as the end times.

Similarly, enemies of the charismatic renewal may be found almost anywhere, but this does not change the reality of their status. The two greatest enemies are "suppression" on the part of some and the "artificial encouragement" by others. This brings back to mind the recognition of the Church by Constantine, which triggered an immediate decline in the strength of the Church and the advent of political maneuvering for petty gain and prominence. For it is a fact of history that "the blood of the martyrs is the seed of the Church!"

Another major problem facing the charismatic renewal is that some of our most able and gifted leaders have become preoccupied with the business of "demon chasing," seeing demons on every door knob and in practically everyone they see. One by one they have made the discovery that God does not honor that activity when it becomes their primary concern. One man, who assured me that I did not know what I was talking about when I minimized the deliverance ministry, later confided to me that "our people are not being healed any more. We are burying them!" Naturally, when you spend more time with the demons than you do with the Lord, He will not honor your prayers for healing. For those who are properly motivated and have a spiritual concern for fellow Christians soon discover the time-wasting futility of chasing demons, and they stop it.

Which is not to say that there are no demons and that we should not deliver people from them, but we should do it in much the same way that Jesus did, as quickly and forcefully as possible, with a minimum of palaver. When Jesus came to a person who was possessed of a demon, He just drove the demon out. He did not get the demon's name, rank and serial number, or stop for a cozy chat; He just drove them out and was done with it. It is a very simple thing.

But there are well-intentioned people who are nonetheless lost in this deliverance ministry, who are making a charicature out of the charismatic renewal. For this reason we classify them as enemies within, and we encourage everyone to pray for them.

Yes, the charismatic renewal is loaded with potential pitfalls. There is hardly a gift that God may give but that it can be misused. God looks on the heart of man, and therein he is revealed to be what he is. Every gift of God, and especially the nine gifts of the Spirit belonging to the baptism with the Holy Spirit, is to be used strictly for the glory of the Lord! Any other use is forbidden. How can they glorify God if we divert them for our own use? Nor can we permit ourselves to become so familiar with these gifts that we become contemptuous.

A great number of people have experienced being "slain in the Spirit." This may be a relatively simple thing where you sink to the floor when the power of the Spirit hits you. Or it can be a very dramatic experience where you may be out for some time or you may have an out-of-the-body experience.

Some people receive the baptism with the Holy Spirit in an experience of this kind. When you try to describe such an experience as this, you find that words are not quite adequate. The results can be so varied as to mislead people by trying to come up with an adequate description. Of course, we are dealing with the Lord and some of His more supernatural work, and this insures a certain amount of mystery.

The point here is to emphasize the fact that this is one of God's unique ways of imparting some spiritual gift. We can misuse the "slain in the Spirit" experience when we use it as some kind of parlor game.

"Submission" is a word that comes up in charismatic circles these days. Properly understood and prayerfully and carefully exercised this, of course, is in keeping the great plan of God in many lives. But, there is that which is a perversion of the word "submission," when someone or a small group seek to foist their will on someone to make them subject unto them. This opens up a pandora's box of perversion, confusion, and frustration for any person who has been called of God to perform a task or mission for God.

There are plenty of examples in Scripture where men have sought by "playing God" or a "prophet" to control situations to suit their ends. In "seeking the will of the Lord," there are often situations where the same man will come up with a loud "Yes" one day and a definite "No" the next.

We may be sure that God is not confused or mixed up. His answers are straightforward, true, and unwavering! They do not change from day to day! He has His plans laid out for us, and we may walk those ways with complete confidence.

We say this with great conviction because we have seen and heard from those who have been immobilized by a confusion of directives which others have assured them come from God. "It is the will of God!" carries weight among God's people.

Every so often we hear a message "from the Lord" being delivered to the group which smacks horribly of being a "sermon" delivered in unkindly fashion to some of the members of the prayer group. Some of these have been challenged and corrected, but everyone is hesitant in the matter of judgment lest they "quench the Spirit" in that individual.

So, to avoid laying the groundwork for the

establishment of "judges" in our groups, we can be doubly helpful by not giving a message unless and until we are compelled to do it. Those who have had the experience of delivering a message to the group from the Lord can enlighten you if you are curious; or if the Lord selects you to deliver a message, you will know whether it be from the Lord, and He wants it delivered. We do not walk in a vacuum, nor do we deal with an uninterested God. He will let you know with unerring accuracy! There is no need for great anxiety—just "wait on the Lord!"

It has been a constant source of amazement to see how similar the leading of the Lord has been in prayer groups all over Scandinavia and Germany as well as in Canada and the United States. The similarity and uniformity is of course tremendously reassuring, proving that it *is* God doing it. And it *is* uncanny; by shutting one's eyes, one can easily imagine himself as being in any one of a hundred prayer groups!

We started this chapter by saying that no one can deny the fact that we are in the end times. Let us close it (and the book) by thinking a little more on that. The most closely guarded secret of all time is the day and the hour of Christ's second coming. The disciples and the followers of Christ started looking shortly after He ascended, and every generation since then has had an eye on the sky.

The attitude of those awaiting His appearing

is no more beautifully presented than in the book *The Robe* by Lloyd Douglas. As the people of that time went about their daily round of activity, whenever they came to the top of a hill, they would look expectantly, hoping to see again the best Friend the world ever had. When they came to a bend in the road, they would hasten their steps just a little, wanting to see Jesus! But, they died without seeing the fulfillment of the prophecy concerning Christ's return.

Two thousand years is a long time to wait. Some have lost interest completely; and when a reminder is given that the end time is near, most people dismiss it by saying, "Oh, they have been saying that for two thousand years!"

But Matthew 24:4-31 is still the best presentation of what we can soon expect and are even now beginning to experience. "Jesus said unto them, Take heed that no man deceive you. For many shall come in my name, saying, I am Christ; and shall deceive many. And ye shall hear of wars and rumors of wars: see that ye be not troubled: for all these things must come to pass, but the end is not yet. For nation shall rise against nation, and kingdom against kingdom; and there shall be famines, and pestilences, and earthquakes, in divers places. All these are the beginning of sorrows. Then shall they deliver you up to be afflicted, and shall kill you: and ye shall be hated of all nations for my name's sake. And then shall many be offended, and shall betray one another, and shall hate one another. And many false prophets shall rise, and shall deceive many. And because iniquity shall abound, the love of many shall wax cold. But he that shall endure unto the end, the same shall be saved. And this gospel of the kingdom shall be preached in all the world for a witness unto all nations; and then shall the end come.

"When ye, therefore, shall see the abomination of desolation, spoken of by Daniel the prophet, stand in the holy place, (whoso readeth, let him understand:). Then let them which be in Judea flee into the mountains: let him which is on the housetop not come down to take anything out of his house: neither let him which is in the field return back to take his clothes. And woe unto them that are with child, and to them that give suck in those days!

"But pray ye that your flight be not in the winter, neither on the Sabbath day; for then shall be great tribulation, such as was not since the beginning of the world to this time, no, nor ever shall be. And except those days should be shortened, there should no flesh be saved: but for the elect's sake those days shall be shortened. Then, if any man shall say unto you, Lo, here is Christ, or, there; believe it not. For there shall arise false Christs, and false prophets, and shall shew great signs and wonders; insomuch that, if it were possible they shall deceive the very elect. Behold, I have told you before. Wherefore if they shall say unto you, Behold, he is in the desert; go not forth: behold, he is in the secret chambers; believe it not. For as the lightning cometh out of the east, and shineth even unto the west; so shall also the coming of the Son of man be. For whereso-ever the carcase is, there will the eagles be gathered together.

"Immediately after the tribulation of those days shall the sun be darkened, and the moon shall not give her light, and the stars shall fall from heaven, and the powers of the heavens shall be shaken: and then shall appear the sign of the Son of man in heaven: and then shall all the tribes of the earth mourn, and they shall see the Son of man coming in the clouds of heaven with power and great glory. And he shall send his angels with a great sound of a trumpet, and they shall gather together his elect from the four winds, from one end of heaven to the other!"

This is the story of the end times according to Jesus Christ. There is no higher authority, and no corrections will be made on this rather simple picture of His coming.

People have been caught up in this fascinating subject, and there has been a veritable flood of books on the market. It may well be that no man knows how many books have been written, but all of it has to come from this scripture passage or a similar one. And the fact remains: no man knows!

In the end, what purpose does further speculation serve? We have no choice but to serve the same purpose of Christ, when He announced the coming of the end times. There will be an end of everything. Our time here on this planet is limited. We have a commission from God to share the Gospel of Jesus Christ with all men to prepare them for the end. God has so graciously provided for us a choice as to our destiny. Jesus said in John's Gospel, 14:1: "Let not your heart be troubled: ye believe in God, believe also in me. In my Father's house are many mansions: if it were not so, I would have told you. I go to prepare a place for you. And if I go and prepare a place for you, I will come again, and receive you unto myself; that where I am, there ye may be also. And whither I go ye know, and the way ye know."

The end times were never intended by Christ to be a time of fear. It is the end of the old and the beginning of the new. And indication of the difference between the two is shown very clearly in Revelation 7:13-17, "And one of the elders answered, saying unto me, What are these which are arrayed in white robes? and whence came they? And I said unto him, Sir, thou knowest. And he said to me, These are they which came out of great tribulation, and have washed their robes, and made them white in the blood of the Lamb. Therefore are they before the throne of God, and serve him day and night in his temple: and he that sitteth on the throne shall dwell among them. They shall hunger no more, neither thirst any more; neither shall the sun light on them, nor any heat. For the Lamb which is in the midst of the throne shall feed them, and shall lead them unto living fountains of waters: and God shall wipe away all tears from their eyes."

Ours is a happy prospect, and the end times are as welcome as they are promising and beautiful. No child of God can legitimately stand in fear and trembling at the prospects of our day. We stand on the tiptoe of expectancy, thrilled and excited at the prospect. Praise the Lord!